Soups

THE FOOD LOVER'S
GUIDE TO SOUPS

SOUPS

THE FOOD LOVER'S GUIDE TO SOUPS

THUNDER BAY
P·R·E·S·S

Published in the United States by
Thunder Bay Press,
An imprint of the Advantage Publishers Group
5880 Oberlin Drive
San Diego, CA 92121-4794
www.advantagebooksonline.com

Copyright © Quantum Books 2000

QUMBCSP

ISBN 1-57145-237-0

Library of Congress Cataloging-in-Publication Data available upon request.

1 2 3 4 5 00 01 02 03 04

This book is produced by
Quantum Books
The Old Brewery, 6 Blundell Street
London N7 9BH

Designer: Bruce Low
Editor: Sarah King

This book was compiled using material from:
Gourmet Soups and The Super Soups Cookbook

Manufactured in Singapore by Master Image
Printed in Singapore by Star Standard Industries Pte. Ltd.

warming meal to combat the chill of winter, while a chilled soup can be a tasty and refreshing dish for a hot summer's day. Many of the soups are filling enough to make a delicious main course, as well as an appetizer.

The soups in this book include both easy-to-prepare recipes such as simple broths

and stocks, as well as more advanced recipes requiring more preparation and cooking time. Imaginative cooks can create mouth-watering soups for every occasion,

and by experimentin[g] ingredients they can cre[ate] twists on the recipes pre[sented].

One of the important [factors of the] soups chosen for this coll[ection is their] nutritional value. Mo[st recipes] recommend using fresh in[gredients] –although frozen alternat[ives are] often suggested – and [most] utilize homemade stocks fo[r the] freshest, healthiest taste. Although ready-made stocks or packet mixes can be substituted, both the flavor and the nutritional benefits of the soups are enhanced by the use of freshly made stock. It is also more enjoyable to prepare and serve a soup that is truly 'home-made'!

Another distinctive feature of these recipes is the imaginative use of a wide range of ingredients to provide different, often exotic, flavors. Drawing on traditional soup recipes from around the world, including Europe, Eastern Europe, Latin America and

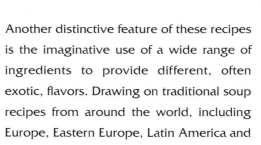

Erma
Wash Sheet'n
Quilt
Love Black + White
pillow case
make Soup together
+ 99¢ store

get mail for   Not to forget
food stamps   28th
Zeroy? Call El!   NEE to make
                    appt asap
                    ON till life to
                    go   4:30 - 5:00

the Orient, there are a delicious variety of tastes that will appeal to even the most jaded of palates.

Many of the soups featured in this book can be prepared in advance, and may well actually improve on reheating. However it is important to reheat soups gently, as some ingredients may be susceptible to overcooking. Another point to remember is that soups should either be ice cold or piping hot – there is nothing quite as unappealing as a lukewarm soup.

Another bonus with soups is that they require little in the way of equipment. A variety of saucepans and casseroles are useful, including at least one with 10 cups/3 1/5 pint capacity. Stainless steel or enamel pans are best, as aluminium is prone to discoloration.

Sharp knives are essential for the preparation of ingredients, as are chopping boards. To prevent raw meat contaminating other ingredients, you should have at least two boards, and keep each for its own use. Peelers, scissors and spoons, including a slotted spoon, are useful, and a skimmer is handy for removing scum or froth from the top of broths and stocks. A ladle is ideal for serving. Several recipes also require a sieve or colander. A blender or food processor is used in some recipes for making a puree. Although a hand-held

electric mixer or food mill can also be used, they are more time-consuming.

Soups are simple and satisfying to prepare, and the recipes in this book range in difficulty from simple broths to more advanced and exotic soups. All cooks will enjoy creating these delicious dishes, and their guests will certainly enjoy the end results!

OVEN TEMPERATURES GUIDE		
C	F	Gas Mark
240	475	9
230	450	8
220	425	7
200	400	6
190	375	5
180	350	4
165	325	3
150	300	2
140	275	1
125	250	1/2
110	225	1/4

Contents

••••

INTRODUCTION

Soups feature in most of the cuisines throughout the world, providing as they do a delicious and sustaining meal that can be prepared cheaply and with relative ease. Over the centuries, most countries and cultures have developed traditional recipes, each with their own distinctive blend of flavors and ingredients.

Historically, soups were originally no more than broths flavored with whatever ingredients were readily available – generally vegetables, with meat being often an expensive luxury. In fact the word supper derives from the word souper, meaning, "to take soup", as soup was traditionally eaten as the evening meal. However, over the years soups have evolved to the point where soup recipes today can be as complex and inventive as any gourmet meal.

The beauty of soups is that they can be made with virtually anything, from leftovers to the most expensive and luxurious of ingredients. The soups featured in this book use a wide variety of ingredients, ranging from fresh vegetables and cheap cuts of meat, to game birds, oysters and lobster.

Both hot and cold soups are included, making this book ideal whatever the weather. A hot soup can provide a hearty,

CHAPTER ONE

STOCKS & VEGETABLES

SIMPLE YET TASTY STOCKS AND
BROTHS PLUS A SELECTION OF
TEMPTING HOT VEGETABLE
SOUPS FROM AROUND
THE WORLD.

INGREDIENTS

2.7-3.2 kg/6–7 lb meaty bones and meat (including veal or other bones, bones from roasts, poultry carcasses and/or poultry necks, giblets, etc)

2 large unpeeled onions, halved and root end trimmed

2 carrots, scrubbed and cut in large pieces

2 leeks, cut in large pieces

1–2 parsnips, cut in large pieces (optional)

2–4 unpeeled garlic cloves, lightly crushed

large bouquet garni (parsley, thyme sprigs, celery leaves, and bay leaf)

3–4 cloves (optional)

6–8 all-spice berries (optional)

STOCK RECIPES

MAKES ABOUT 10 CUPS/3 l/5 PT

Use the following stock recipes as a framework for stock-making. Make smaller or larger batches or vary the ingredients, if you wish, but be sure to use enough ingredients in your stock to give good flavor or it will need to be reduced to concentrate the flavor and some of the volume will be lost.

Meat Stock

A variety of ingredients may be used in making meat stock. Veal bones give more flavor than beef bones, but if the bones have no meat on them, it is best to add some stewing beef. You can also use a meaty cut such as shank, or add some chicken necks, backs, or carcasses to provide gelatin. Avoid lamb bones unless you want to make lamb stock.

Put the bones and meat, the onions, carrots, celery, leeks, parsnips, if using, and garlic in a large stockpot or heavy pan, pushing the vegetables down between the bones. Cover with cold water by at least 2 inches and bring to a boil over medium-high heat. As the liquid heats, foam will begin to appear on the surface. As soon as it appears and until it stops surfacing, skim off the foam with a slotted spoon.

When the stock reaches boiling point, reduce the heat to low and add the *bouquet garni* and spices, if using. Simmer very slowly, uncovered, for four to five hours, skimming occasionally and topping up with cold water if the liquid level falls below the solids. Gently ladle the stock through a strainer, lined with damp cheesecloth if you wish, into a large container.

To remove the fat, chill the stock to allow it to congeal, then scrape off the fat. Gently remove any further traces of fat by wiping a paper towel lightly across the surface. If time is short, use a fat separator to remove the fat from the warm stock or spoon off the fat. Blot any remaining beads of fat with paper towels.

If you wish, reduce the stock to concentrate the flavor. Store in the refrigerator or freezer.

Brown Stock

Put the bones, meat, and vegetables in a large roasting pan and brown in a preheated 230°C/450°F oven for 30 to 40 minutes, turning occasionally. Transfer the ingredients to the stockpot, discarding the fat, and add the bouquet garni, cloves, and all-spice berries. Proceed as for Meat Stock.

CHICKEN STOCK

MAKES ABOUT 8 CUPS / 2.4 l / 4 PT

Chicken bones are more readily available than meat bones, so chicken stock is easier—as well as quicker—to make. If you want cooked chicken meat for your soup, use a whole boiling fowl or roasting chicken.

Proceed as for Meat Stock, but simmer for only 2 to 3 hours. If using a whole bird or pieces, cut off the breast meat after 25 to 30 minutes and return the remainder to the stockpot.

VARIATIONS
Turkey Stock

Remove any stuffing, break or chop the carcass into pieces, and, if you wish, add sage leaves to the bouquet garni. Proceed as for Chicken Stock.

Game Stock

Proceed as for Chicken Stock, with or without initial browning.

INGREDIENTS

1.8-2 kg/4–4½ lb raw chicken backs, necks, or raw or cooked carcasses, or whole or cut up chicken

2 large unpeeled onions, root end trimmed

3 carrots, scrubbed, cut in large pieces

1 celery stalk, cut in large pieces

1 leek, cut in large pieces

2 unpeeled garlic cloves, lightly crushed

large *bouquet garni* (parsley, thyme, and marjoram or tarragon sprigs, and bay leaf)

FISH STOCK

MAKES ABOUT 6 CUPS / 1.8 l / 3 PT

Fish stock is quick and easy to make. The initial cooking of the fish parts in butter makes a richer stock, but if you wish, omit this step and combine all the ingredients in the stockpot. Avoid using the bones of oily fish, such as mackerel or salmon, for all-purpose stock.

Melt the butter in a large nonreactive pan or flameproof casserole over medium-high heat and add the fish parts. Cook for 2 to 3 minutes and add the vegetables, wine, water, parsley, and peppercorns.

Bring to a boil, skimming off any foam that rises to the top. Reduce the heat to low and simmer gently for 25 minutes. Ladle the stock through a strainer lined with cheesecloth and remove any fat.

INGREDIENTS

1 Tbsp butter

1 kg/2 lb heads, bones, and trimmings from fresh white fish

1 onion, sliced thin

1 carrot, sliced thin

1 leek, sliced thin

1 cup/240 ml/8 floz dry white wine

5 cups/1.2 l/2 pt water

6–8 parsley sprigs

6–8 black peppercorns

INGREDIENTS

225-450 kg/½–1 lb shrimp, or lobster shells,
heads,
and legs
1 onion, chopped
1 small carrot, sliced
1 celery stalk, sliced
½ lemon, sliced thin
6 cups/1.8 l/3 pt water
bouquet garni (parsley, thyme, sprigs, and
leek greens)

SHELLFISH STOCK
MAKES ABOUT 6 CUPS/1.8 l/3 PT

Don't throw away the shells of crustaceans. Make this stock with the shells of shrimps, or lobster you have enjoyed for another meal.

Combine the shellfish shells and parts with the vegetables, lemon, water, and *bouquet garni* in a large pan. Bring to a boil, skimming off any foam as it rises to the top.

Reduce the heat to low and simmer, partially covered, for 25 minutes. Ladle the stock through a strainer lined with cheesecloth and remove any fat.

INGREDIENTS

1 large onion, halved and sliced thin
2 shallots, sliced thin
1 parsnip, sliced thin
1 large leek, sliced thin
1–2 turnips or ½ rutabaga, halved and
sliced thin
1 potato, cut in large chunks
50-75 g/2–3 oz mushrooms or mushroom
stalks
50-75 g/2–3 oz green beans or green bean
trimmings (optional)
150-175 g/5–6 oz cabbage, or 75-100 g/
3–4 oz other greens, such as lettuce, chard,
or kale
large bouquet garni (parsley, thyme and
marjoram sprigs, a few rosemary or sage
leaves, and 1–2 bay leaves)

VEGETABLE STOCK
MAKES ABOUT 8 CUPS/1.8 l/4 PT

With vegetable stock, it is even more important to balance the proportion of water to ingredients and to give thought to the eventual use of the stock so you can select suitable ingredients.

Combine the ingredients in a large stockpot, add cold water to cover by at least 1 inch/2.5 cm. Bring to a boil over medium-high heat, skimming off any foam as it rises to the top.

Reduce the heat to low and simmer gently for about 45 minutes. Ladle the stock through a strainer lined with cheesecloth and remove any fat.

SPICED VEGETABLE STOCK

MAKES ABOUT 6 CUPS/1.8 l/3 PT

This Indian-spiced stock makes a good base for curried soups or stews.

Heat the oil in a large heavy pan or stockpot over medium heat. Add the onion, leek, carrots, and celery, and cook until the onion becomes softer and slightly transparent. Add the spices and dried herbs, and continue cooking for 2 to 3 minutes.

Stir in the water, parsley, and lemon, and bring to a boil. Reduce the heat to low and simmer for 30 to 40 minutes. Strain the stock and remove any fat.

INGREDIENTS

1 Tbsp vegetable oil

1 large onion, sliced

1 large leek, sliced

2 carrots, chopped

1 celery stalk with leaves, sliced

2 garlic cloves, peeled and crushed

1 tsp cilantro seeds

3 cardamom pods

2 cloves

½ tsp each cumin seed and mustard seed

½ tsp each dried thyme and oregano

6 cups/1.8 l/3 pt water

6–8 parsley sprigs

½ lemon (unwaxed or scrubbed), thinly sliced

GARLIC STOCK

MAKES ABOUT 6 CUPS/1.8 l/3 PT

This herb and garlic infusion is a basic vegetable stock that you can make quickly with ingredients you are likely to have on hand.

Combine the water, garlic, thyme, marjoram, and bay leaf in a saucepan.

Bring to a boil, reduce the heat to medium-low, and simmer, partially covered for 30 to 45 minutes then strain.

INGREDIENTS

6 cups/1.8 l/3 pt water

about 20 garlic cloves, unpeeled

4–6 thyme sprigs, or ½ tsp dried thyme

6 marjoram sprigs, or ½ tsp dried marjoram

Bay leaf

INGREDIENTS

4 inch/10 cm piece dried kelp (*konbu*), wiped with a damp cloth

6 cups/1.8 1/3 pt water water

3 cups bonito flakes (*katsuo-bushi*)

PREMIER DASHI
MAKES ABOUT 6 CUPS/1.81/3PT

First, make two or three cuts about 1 inch/10 cm long in the kelp to release more flavor, then put the water and kelp into a pan and place on a low flame. Remove the kelp just before the water begins to boil.

Add the bonito flakes when the liquid comes back to a boil and turn off the heat. Leave the liquid until the flakes sink to the bottom of the pan, then strain through a cheesecloth or paper filter. Retain the bonito flakes and kelp for preparing standard *dashi*.

INGREDIENTS

1 Tbsp sesame oil

½-inch/1 cm piece fresh ginger root, peeled and chopped fine

1 garlic clove, chopped fine

1 scallion, chopped fine

4 Tbsp Chinese rice wine or Japanese *sake*

3 Tbsp light soy sauce

2 Tbsp sugar

8 Tbsp red *miso* paste

2 tsp chili oil

6 cups/1.8 1/3 pt water chicken stock

MISO BROTH
MAKES 6 CUPS/1.81/3PT

Heat the oil in a pan. Add the ginger, garlic, and scallion, then fry for 30 seconds. Add the wine first, then soy sauce, sugar, *miso* paste, and chili oil, and mix together. Add the chicken stock, and bring to a boil. Remove from the heat.

DIPPING BROTH

MAKES ABOUT 3 CUPS/180ML/1 ½ PT

¾ cup/180 ml/6 floz mirin
2¼ cups/540 ml/18 floz premier dashi
¾ cup/180 ml/6 floz Japanese soy sauce

Put the mirin in a pan, and bring to a boil. Add the dashi and soy sauce and simmer for 3 to 4 minutes; then remove from the heat and chill.

Dipping broth can be stored refrigerated in a jar for 3 to 4 days.

STANDARD DASHI

MAKES ABOUT 6 CUPS/1.8l/3PT

6 cups/1.8 l/ 3 pt water
used kelp and bonito flakes from premier dashi

This recipe recycles bonito flakes and kelp used in making Premier Japanese Dashi. It is used in the same way.

Put the water, kelp, and bonito flakes in a large pan. Bring to a boil over a low heat, and simmer gently for 5 minutes. Skim off any scum that forms on the surface.

Strain through a cheesecloth or a coffee filter.

INGREDIENTS

550 g/1¼ lb chicken bones, chopped rough

100 g/¼ lb pork bones

1 small onion, cut in half

1 small leek, cut in half diagonally

2 fat garlic cloves, lightly crushed

1 inch/2.5 cm piece ginger root, peeled and sliced

10 cups/3 l/5 pt water

ORIENTAL CHICKEN STOCK
MAKES 7-8 CUPS/2-2.4l/3½ PT

Used to make Chinese and Ramen hot noodle soups and Chinese sauces.

Wash the bones before use. Blanch the chicken and pork bones in boiling water for 2 minutes. Rinse.

Put the bones, onion, leek, garlic, ginger, and water in a pan. Bring to a boil, and simmer for 1 hour, skimming off the scum occasionally. After an hour, strain the stock through a fine mesh strainer or cheesecloth.

INGREDIENTS

6 cups/1.8 l/3 pt chicken stock

2 tsp salt

4 tsp Chinese rice wine or Japanese *sake*

2 tsp shortening

4 Tbsp light soy sauce

4 tsp dark soy sauce

ground black pepper

SOY SAUCE BROTH
MAKES 6 CUPS/1.8l/3PT

Put the stock, salt, wine, and shortening in a pan. Bring to a boil, and simmer for 2 to 3 minutes.

Turn off the heat, add the light and dark soy sauce, black pepper, and stir.

LIGHT CHICKEN STOCK

MAKES ABOUT 6 CUPS/1.8I/3PT

INGREDIENTS

9½ cups /2.25 l/3¾ pt water

3 chicken drumsticks

Used for Thai, Indonesian, Malaysian and hot noodle dishes.

Put the water and chicken drumsticks in a saucepan, bring to a boil, and simmer for about 40 minutes. When the meat on the drumstick shin begins to fall away, exposing the bone, the stock should be ready.

Strain through a metal strainer, and reserve the drumstick meat as a topping for a noodle dish.

FRENCH ONION SOUP

SERVES 6

Believe it or not, this soup is the traditional French pick-me-up for the early morning after the night before! The flavor is supposed to galvanize you back into life.

Cook the onions in the butter and oil over high heat in a flameproof casserole dish until softened and well browned, this may take up to 10 minutes.

Stir the flour into the onions and then cook gently for 1 to 2 minutes. Remove from the heat and gradually add the stock stirring all the time, then season lightly, and add the bay leaves. Return the casserole dish to the heat and bring the soup gradually to a boil, then cover, and simmer for 45 minutes. The soup should be a rich, dark brown color.

Preheat the broiler. Remove the bay leaves and season the soup to taste. Drop the slices of bread into the soup, one per serving, then scatter the cheese over the bread. Cook under the hot broiler until the cheese has melted and is bubbling. Serve immediately, with one slice of bread in each portion.

INGREDIENTS

2 medium onions, sliced

1 Tbsp butter

2 Tbsp olive oil

2 Tbsp fine whole-wheat flour

3 cups/720 ml/1 pt 4 floz well-flavored vegetable stock

salt and ground black pepper

3 bay leaves

4–6 slices whole-wheat baguette

MISO RAMEN WITH CORN

SERVES 4

The miso *broth used in this dish has a sweet, spicy flavor. The taste of the broth will differ depending on the variety of miso used. Once you have prepared the tasty broth, this simple and quick ramen dish is ready to eat in minutes. For an easy variation, try a pat of butter dropped onto the noodles to enrich the taste.*

Boil plenty of water in a pan. Add the noodles, and cook over a medium heat for 3 minutes. Drain, and divide into individual bowls.

Heat the *miso* broth. Pile the corn onto the noodles, then add the sprouts, scallions, and *nori*. Gently pour the miso broth over the top, and serve at once.

INGREDIENTS

450g/1 lb ramen noodles, or
350 g/³/₄ lb dried thin egg noodles
6 cups/1.8 l/3 pt *miso* broth (see page 16)

Topping

1 cup/100 g/4 oz canned corn
a handful of alfalfa sprouts
3 scallions, chopped
½ sheet nori seaweed, cut in 4

23

INGREDIENTS

2 garlic cloves, chopped fine

¼ tsp each dried thyme and marjoram

3–4 Tbsp olive oil

900 g/2 lb ripe tomatoes, cored and sliced thick

1 medium onion, chopped

salt and ground black pepper

1¼ cups/300 ml/½ pt vegetable or chicken stock

Goat cheese croutons

3 oz/75g firm goat cheese (slightly smaller in diameter than the bread), cut in 4 slices

ROASTED TOMATO SOUP WITH GOAT CHEESE CROUTONS

SERVES 4

Roasting the tomatoes and other vegetables gives this soup added flavor, essential if using winter tomatoes.

Preheat a 170°C/375°F oven. Mix together the garlic and herbs. Drizzle a tablespoonful of the olive oil in the bottom of a large shallow baking dish. Layer the tomatoes, onions, and garlic-herb mixture in two or three layers. Drizzle each layer as you go with the olive oil and season with a little salt and pepper. Bake, uncovered, for 25 minutes, or until all the vegetables are soft.

Work the vegetables through a food mill fitted with a fine blade set over a pan. Skim off any standing oil. Add the stock or water and simmer over medium heat, stirring occasionally, for about 15 minutes, or until heated through. Taste and adjust the seasoning, if necessary.

For the goat cheese croutons, preheat the broiler. Toast the bread lightly on both sides under the broiler. Top with slices of goat cheese and broil until lightly browned.

Ladle the soup into warm shallow bowls and place a crouton in each. Serve immediately.

MISO RAMEN WITH SHREDDED LEEK

SERVES 4

Noodles in miso *broth are one of the most popular noodle dishes served in Japan. It is essential to use a good quality miso paste as this provides the crucial sweet and salty flavoring to the dish. The shredded leek should have a firm, supple texture, so if prepared beforehand, soak it in a little water to prevent it from drying out.*

Bring some water to a boil in a pan, and blanch the spinach for 1 to 2 minutes. Rinse, drain, and divide into four equal portions.

Bring more water to a boil in a large pan. Add the noodles, and boil for 4 minutes. Drain, and divide among individual serving bowls.

Heat the *miso* broth for 2 to 3 minutes. Pile the leek, spinach, and bamboo shoots on top of the noodles. Add the miso broth, and serve.

INGREDIENTS

225 g/½ lb fresh spinach

450 g/1 lb ramen noodles, or 375 g/14 oz fresh or 350 g/¾ lb dried egg noodles

6 cups/1.8 l/3 pt miso broth (see page 16)

4-inch/10 cm piece of leek, cut in four pieces and shredded

4 Tbsp cooked dried bamboo shoots (*shinachiku*) (optional)

INGREDIENTS

25 g/1 oz butter

1½ cups/300 g/12 oz chopped onions

½ cup/100 g/4 oz chopped scallions

3 bunches watercress

4 potatoes, peeled, cooked, and diced

3 cups/720 ml/24 floz chicken stock

1 tsp lemon juice

2 tsp dried dill, or 1 Tbsp fresh

¼ tsp white pepper

½ tsp paprika

1 cup/200 g/8 oz heavy cream

salt, to taste

CREAM OF WATERCRESS SOUP

SERVES 4

Watercress is a tasty, peppery green that often grows wild. It brings a wonderful flavor to this rich cream soup.

Melt the butter in heavy pan. Sauté the onions and scallions over low heat until light gold, 20 to 25 minutes.

Meanwhile, clean the watercress. Immerse in at least two baths of clean water and rinse well. Remove the leaves and tender stems, and discard the tough stems.

Add the watercress to the onions and sauté for 5 minutes. Add the potato, 1 cup of chicken stock, the lemon juice and dill. Simmer for 5 minutes. Let cool slightly. Purée in batches in a blender or food processor.

Pour the purée back into the pan. Add the remaining chicken stock, pepper, and paprika. Bring to a boil. Add the cream. Warm until just barely at boiling point. Taste, and add salt if needed.

PARSNIP AND APPLE SOUP

SERVES 4–6

Curried parsnip is one of the new generation of classic soups. Add a cooking apple to the mixture if you like — its sharpness gives a real punch to the flavor of the soup.

Cook the onion in the oil for 4 to 5 minutes until soft, then stir in the curry powder with the parsnips. Cook for a further 2 to 3 minutes before adding the apple and stock. Bring to a boil, then simmer for 30 minutes or until the parsnip is soft.

Allow the soup to cool slightly, then purée until smooth in a blender or food processor. Rinse the pan and return the soup to it, adding sufficient water to thin the soup if necessary. Reheat gently, then season to taste with salt and pepper. Add the lemon juice just before serving and garnish with parsley or cilantro.

INGREDIENTS

1 onion, chopped
1 Tbsp sunflower oil
1 tsp mild curry powder
450 g/1 lb parsnips, chopped
1 cooking apple, peeled, cored, and sliced
5 cups/1.2 1/2 pt well-flavored vegetable stock
salt and ground black pepper
juice of ½ lemon
chopped fresh parsley or cilantro, to garnish

BUTTERNUT SQUASH SOUP

SERVES 4 – 6

This versatile soup can be made with different kinds of squashes, including acorn and zucchini, so you can enjoy it throughout the year. The buttermilk adds a creamy, slightly tangy flavor rather than a sharp, identifiable buttermilk taste. However, if you really dislike buttermilk, you can substitute heavy cream. To save time, bake the squash the night before you plan to serve the soup.

Preheat a 180°C/350°F oven. Cut the squash in half lengthwise, and brush the flesh with olive oil. Bake until tender, about 45 minutes. Let it cool slightly. Scoop out the pulp.

In a heavy pan, sauté the leeks in butter for 10 minutes. Add the squash, stock, and seasonings. Bring to a boil and simmer for 10 minutes.

In two or three batches, purée the soup in a blender or food processor. Return the soup to a medium heat and gradually bring to a boil. Add the buttermilk and heat, but do not let the soup boil. Add salt to taste.

INGREDIENTS

2 medium butternut squash

1–2 Tbsp olive oil

3 Tbsp butter

3 cups/720 ml/24 floz chicken stock

2 leeks, chopped, white part only

¼ tsp white pepper

½ tsp dried oregano

½ tsp dried thyme

1 cup/240 ml/8 floz buttermilk

salt, to taste

BUCKWHEAT AND MUSHROOM SOUP

SERVES 6

Buckwheat has a strong, slightly sweet, and fragrantly nutty flavor. It is often the principal ingredient of simple rustic soups and stews, but in this more luxurious recipe, it blends with fresh and dried mushrooms to produce a very creamy soup. Only a little buckwheat is required to achieve a subtle flavoring.

Soak the ceps in the sherry for at least 30 minutes before starting the soup. Heat the butter and the oil together, then add the onion, celery, and bacon, and cook slowly for about 5 minutes, until the vegetables have softened but not browned.

Add the chopped mushrooms and garlic and cook slowly for a further 2 to 3 minutes, until the juices start to run from the mushrooms. Add the ceps and the sherry, then stir in the buckwheat and pour in the stock.

Bring the soup slowly to a boil, stirring up any sediment from the bottom of the pan. Season lightly with the salt, pepper, and grated nutmeg then cover the pan and gently simmer the soup for 40 minutes.

Allow the soup to cool slightly then purée until smooth in a blender or food processor. Rinse the pan and return the soup to it with the milk. Reheat gently then season to taste. Garnish with a swirl of cream and a little paprika before serving in warmed soup bowls with warm crusty bread.

INGREDIENTS

25 g/1 oz dried cep mushrooms

generous 1 cup/240 ml/8 floz sherry

1 Tbsp butter

1 Tbsp olive oil

1 onion, chopped fine

2 celery stalks, chopped fine

2 slices Canadian bacon, chopped fine

250 g/9 oz mushrooms, chopped rough

2 plump garlic cloves, sliced fine

50 g/1¾ oz raw buckwheat groats

5 cups/1.2 1/2 pt well-flavored vegetable stock

salt and ground black pepper

grated fresh nutmeg

1¼ cups/300 ml/½ pt milk

INGREDIENTS

2 ham hocks

1 medium onion, peeled and quartered

2 celery stalks, cut into 3 inch/7.5 cm pieces

2 carrots, cut into 3 inch/7.5 cm pieces

several sprigs of fresh parsley

1 bay leaf

3 cups/720 ml/24 floz chicken stock

4–5 ears corn

½ tsp cumin

⅛ tsp cayenne pepper

⅛ tsp white pepper

1 cup/240 ml/8 floz cream

½ cup/50 g/2 oz chopped scallions

½ small sweet red bell pepper, chopped

HAM AND CORN CHOWDER

SERVES 4–6

Ham and corn, such integral parts of Southern cuisine are combined in this inexpensive corn chowder. Use fresh corn if it's available, or frozen if not. The last-minute addition of scallions and red bell peppers adds crunch and color.

Place the ham hocks, onion, celery, carrots, parsley, and bay leaf in a large pan, and cover with water. Bring to a boil and simmer about 1½ hours. Remove the ham hocks, and cut off the meat. Return the bones to the pot, and continue reducing the stock. Cut the ham meat into slivers.

Strain the ham stock and discard the vegetables. Combine 1 cup of the ham in a large pan with 3 cups chicken stock. Bring to a boil. Add the corn, the slivered ham, and the spices, and simmer for 20 minutes. Add the cream, scallions, and red bell peppers and bring just barely to boiling point. Taste and adjust for seasoning. The ham is salty and should provide enough salt. Serve on warmed soup plates with crusty bread.

BUTTERNUT AND ORANGE SOUP

SERVES 4–6

This soup has South African origins. It is a wonderful combination of flavors and will quickly establish itself as a family favorite. Do not boil the soup after adding the orange juice or the flavor will become slightly tainted.

Cook the onion in the oil until softened but not browned, then add the prepared squash and cook slowly for 5 minutes, stirring occasionally. Stir in the grated orange rind then add the stock, bay leaves, and seasonings. Bring the soup to a boil, then cover, and simmer gently for 40 minutes, until the squash is tender and cooked through.

Allow the soup to cool slightly, remove the bay leaves, then purée in a blender or food processor until smooth. Rinse the pan and return the soup to it, adding the orange juice. Reheat the soup slowly—do not let it boil—then season to taste. Add the chopped fresh parsley just before serving piping hot.

INGREDIENTS

1 onion, chopped

2 Tbsp vegetable oil

1–2 butternut squashes, weighing about 900 g/2 lb, peeled and diced

shredded rind and juice of 2 oranges

7 cups/1.7 l/2¾ pt well-flavored vegetable stock

2 bay leaves

salt and ground black pepper

grated fresh nutmeg

2 Tbsp parsley, chopped fresh

SQUASH CHOWDER

SERVES 6

Use any hard-skinned squash for this chowder. Crown Prince is delicious but acorn will work just as well, although a smoother-skinned squash will be easier to peel.

Cook the squash and the bacon in the oil in a heavy pan for 6 to 8 minutes, until the squash is beginning to soften. Add the herbs and stock, season lightly, then bring to a boil. Reduce the heat and simmer for 10 minutes, then add the cabbage and creamed coconut, and continue cooking for a further 10 to 15 minutes.

Remove the thyme and bay leaves, then add the milk and the chopped tomato with the shrimp, if desired. Return the chowder to a boil for 5 minutes more. Season, then add the vinegar and parsley before serving.

INGREDIENTS

350 g/12 oz Crown Prince squash, diced fine

2 slices Canadian bacon, diced fine

2 Tbsp olive oil

4–5 sprigs fresh thyme

2 bay leaves

3 cups/720 ml/24 floz well-flavored vegetable stock

salt and ground black pepper

1 cup/100 g/4 oz white cabbage, shredded fine

⅓ cup/100 g/4 oz creamed coconut, crumbled or diced

1 cup/240 ml/8 floz milk

1 large tomato, diced fine

1 cup/100 g/4 oz frozen shrimp (optional)

salt and ground black pepper

1 Tbsp white wine vinegar

chopped fresh parsley, to garnish

GARDEN VEGETABLE CHOWDER

SERVES 6–8

INGREDIENTS

2 Tbsp butter

1 onion, chopped

1 shallot, chopped

1 leek, split lengthwise and sliced thin

1–2 garlic cloves, minced

3 Tbsp flour

3 carrots, halved lengthwise and sliced thin

½ small celery root, diced fine, or 2 celery stalks, sliced fine

2 small turnips, diced fine

2 large baking potatoes, diced

3 cups/720 ml/24 floz vegetable or light chicken stock

bouquet garni (thyme and marjoram sprigs, parsley, and bay leaf)

salt and white pepper

1 cup/100 g/4 oz chopped green beans

kernels cut from 2 ears of corn

1⅔ cups/400 ml/14 floz milk

¾ cup/180 ml/6 floz heavy cream

crispy fried onions

The crispy onion garnish gives a pleasant contrast to the creaminess of the soup, but it is equally good topped with shredded Cheddar cheese.

Melt the butter in a large heavy pan over medium heat. Add the onion, shallot, leek, and garlic. Cook until the vegetables start to soften, about 5 minutes, stirring frequently. Stir in the flour and cook for 2 minutes. Add the carrots, celery root or celery, turnips, potatoes, and stock, stirring and scraping the bottom of the pan.

Bring to a boil, stirring frequently. Add the *bouquet garni* and season with salt and pepper. Reduce the heat to medium-low and simmer, stirring occasionally, until the vegetables are almost tender, about 20 minutes.

Stir in the beans, corn, and milk. Continue cooking until the beans are tender, about 10 minutes. Stir in the cream, adjust the seasoning and heat through. Remove the *bouquet garni*. Ladle into warm bowls and garnish with crispy fried onions.

TUSCAN WHITE BEAN AND KALE SOUP

SERVES 6

This soup is perfect for a fireside supper on a winter's evening. Serve it with warm focaccio *or garlic bread.*

Drain the beans, put into a saucepan with cold water to cover and set over high heat. Bring to a boil and boil for 10 minutes. Drain and add fresh cold water to cover. Bring to a boil again, drain and rinse well.

Heat the oil in a large heavy saucepan over medium-high heat and add the pancetta or bacon. Cook until lightly browned, stirring frequently. Remove with a slotted spoon to drain on paper towels and pour off all but 1 tablespoon of the fat. Reduce the heat to low, add the onion, shallot, carrot and garlic, and cook for 3–4 minutes until slightly softened. Add the beans, tomatoes, water, bouquet garni and pancetta or bacon, and simmer until the beans are tender, 1–2 hours. Season to taste with salt and pepper.

Stir in the kale and continue cooking for 15–20 minutes, or until it is tender. Adjust the seasoning and ladle the soup into warm bowls. Serve sprinkled with Parmesan cheese, if you wish.

INGREDIENTS

1¼ cups/125 g/5 oz dried borlotti or navy beans, soaked overnight in cold water to cover generously

1 Tbsp olive oil

90 g/3½ oz pancetta or smoked lean bacon, chopped

1 onion, finely chopped

1 shallot, finely chopped

1 carrot, finely chopped

1–2 garlic cloves, minced

4 tomatoes, peeled, seeded and chopped, or 1¾ cups/175 g/6 oz canned chopped tomatoes

5 cups/2 1/2pt water

bouquet garni (thyme and marjoram sprigs, parsley stems and bay leaf)

100 g/4 oz curly kale leaves, finely chopped (2 lightly packed cups)

freshly grated or shaved Parmesan cheese, for serving (optional)

43

CHEESE AND ONION SOUP

SERVES 4 – 6

Heat the oil in a large pan and gently stir-fry the onions until lightly browned. Add the stock and bring to a boil.

Meanwhile, peel the potatoes and shred them into the pan. Reduce the heat and simmer until the potatoes have cooked and soup has thickened.

Add the shredded cheese, stirring to melt. Season to taste with salt and soy sauce. Serve with whole-wheat bread and a crisp green salad.

INGREDIENTS

1–2 Tbsp oil

2 medium onions, sliced

5 cups/1.2 1/2 pt stock

2 small potatoes

1½ cups/150 g/5 oz shredded Cheddar cheese

salt

soy sauce

INGREDIENTS

1 kg/2¼ lb potatoes, cut into smallish pieces
if large

2 garlic cloves, chopped coarse

9 cups/2.1 l/3½ pt light chicken stock or
water

450 g/1 lb spring cabbage or Savoy cabbage

225 g/8 oz chorizo sausage, sliced (optional)

salt and ground black pepper

4–6 Tbsp olive oil, to serve

1 Tbsp cilantro leaves, to serve (optional)

GREEN SOUP

SERVES 4

This soup comes from Portugal where it is called Caldo Verde. *The secret of a good caldo verde is to shred the leaves extremely finely. With good bread it makes a substantial main course in its own right, but in Portugal it is often served as an appetizer. It keeps well and is just as nice, if not better, reheated.*

Put the potatoes, garlic, and stock or water into a large pan, bring to a boil, and simmer gently for 15 minutes, or until tender.

Meanwhile, remove the stems from the cabbage leaves. Roll the leaves into tubes and then cut across them to shred as thinly as possible.

Mash the potatoes and garlic together in the saucepan to form a fairly smooth purée. Add the cabbage and sausage, if using, and simmer for about 5 minutes, until warmed through. Season to taste.

Ladle into warmed soup bowls and swirl some olive oil into each portion. Scatter over a few cilantro leaves, if using, and serve.

MINTED PEA SOUP

SERVES 6

Pea Soup is one of the great classics. Use frozen peas and just add a little lime for an extra brightness of flavor. The essential ingredients are young peas and fresh mint. This soup is just as good hot or served cold over crushed ice in the summer.

Cook the onion slowly in the butter until soft but not brown; it is important to soften the onion really well as this soup has a very short cooking time. Stir in the peas and the mint, then add the water, and bring the soup to a boil. Simmer for only 3 to 4 minutes, then the peas are just cooked—this will preserve the bright color of the soup.

Cool the soup slightly then add the lime rind and purée until smooth in a blender. Rinse the pan and return the soup to it, seasoning to taste with salt and white pepper. Reheat gently. Serve with a swirl of light cream.

INGREDIENTS

1 small onion, chopped fine
2 Tbsp butter
450 g/1 lb frozen peas
2 Tbsp chopped fresh mint
5 cups/1.2 1/2 pt water
shredded rind of 1 lime
salt and white pepper, to taste
light cream to serve

GREEN "PISTOU" SOUP

SERVES 4

The lovely, all-green color is an unexpected delight—add pasta if you like. To make a classic pistou add a handful of cooked vermicelli, broken into the pot.

Lightly sauté the leek, onion, and garlic in the olive oil until they are soft, then add the tomatoes, seasoning, and sugar, and cook over a medium heat about 10 minutes. Add the vegetable stock and water, the zucchini, potato, and cabbage, and continue to cook over medium heat until the potatoes are just tender and the zucchini are quite soft. The cabbage will be soft by now, too.

Add the white beans, chard or spinach leaves, broccoli, and green beans, and cook for about another 5 minutes, or until the broccoli and green beans are cooked through.

Serve immediately in warmed bowls with a tablespoon or two of pistou stirred in, accompanied by the grated Parmesan sprinkled on top. Do not heat the pistou, or its fragrance will quickly dissipate.

Pistou

Crush the garlic cloves with a mortar and pestle, then transfer to a food processor and continue crushing. Add the basil, then slowly add the olive oil. Add enough olive oil for it to be smooth and oily, then stir in the cheese. Store the pistou in a covered bowl for no longer than two days in a refrigerator.

INGREDIENTS

1 leek, chopped

2 onions, chopped

5 garlic cloves, chopped coarse

3 Tbsp extra virgin olive oil

3 medium-sized ripe, yellow tomatoes, diced

salt and ground black pepper

a pinch of sugar

3½ cups/840 ml/28 floz vegetable stock

3½ cups/840 ml/28 floz water

3 small zucchini, cut into bite-sized pieces

1 medium-sized potato, peeled and diced

¼ cabbage, sliced thin

¾ cup75 g/3 oz fresh, white, shell beans, such as cooked cannellini

8 chard or spinach leaves, sliced thin

¼–½ bunch broccoli, cut into florets

a handful of green beans, cut into bite-sized pieces

1 quantity of pistou (see below)

extra grated Parmesan cheese, to serve

PISTOU

3 garlic cloves, peeled

Several handfuls of fresh, basil leaves, torn

5 Tbsp exra virgin olive oil

6 Tbsp shredded Parmesan cheese

51

INGREDIENTS

450 g/1 lb ramen noodles, or 375 g/14 oz
fresh or 350 g/¾ lb dried thin egg noodles
6 cups1.4 l/2¼ pt soy sauce broth (see page
18)

Topping

2 Tbsp vegetable oil
1 Tbsp sesame oil
1 small onion, sliced
¾ cup/75 g/3 oz snow peas, cut in half
diagonally
2–3 small carrots, cut into long matchsticks
2½ cups/200 g/8 oz bean sprouts
225 g/½ lb Chinese cabbage, chopped
2 dried black ear fungi or dried *shiitake*
mushrooms, soaked in water, rinsed, and
chopped
salt and ground black pepper

RAMEN WITH STIR-FRIED VEGETABLES
SERVES 4

Ramen noodles topped with a blend of fresh and flash-fried vegetables— deliciously simple and simply delicious!

Heat the oils in a wok or frying pan until very hot. Stir-fry the onion, snow peas, and carrots for 2 minutes, then add the bean sprouts, Chinese cabbage, black fungi or mushrooms, and stir-fry for another 3 to 4 minutes. Season with salt and pepper to taste.

Boil plenty of water in a large pan, and add the noodles. Cook for 3 minutes before draining well. Put the noodles into four bowls.

Heat the soy sauce broth. Pile the stir-fried vegetables onto the noodles, and pour the broth over the top.

SUMMER VEGETABLE SOUP

SERVES 6–8

Made from summer vegetables picked at their absolute peak of freshness, this is a light, healthy soup. It is a favorite for a lunch or a late supper.

Prepare and cut the carrots, cauliflower, potatoes, and beans into ¼ inch/½ cm cubes. Place the cubed vegetables with the radishes and peas in a pan, cover with water, and add the salt. Boil, uncovered, for 5 minutes or until tender. Add the spinach and cook for another 5 minutes. Strain the liquid into a bowl and put the vegetables into another bowl.

Melt the butter, remove from the heat and stir in the salt and flour. Slowly add the reserved hot vegetable stock, whisking all the time, then beat in the milk. Mix the egg yolk and cream in a bowl. Whisk ⅔ cup of the hot soup into the egg mixture, spooning it in. Then whisk the warmed egg and cream mixture back into the soup.

Add the vegetables to the soup and reheat. Just before it boils, add the shrimp and simmer for 3 to 4 minutes. Stir in the white pepper. Serve with chopped dill or parsley.

INGREDIENTS

4 small carrots

1 small cauliflower

2 new potatoes

225 g/8 oz green beans

4 small radishes, halved

175 g/6 oz peas

100 g/4 oz fresh spinach, washed

2 Tbsp butter

2 tsp salt

2 Tbsp flour

⅓ cup/80 ml/3 floz milk

1 egg yolk

¼ cup/60 ml/2 floz heavy cream

MINESTRONE SOUP

SERVES 4–6

There are many versions of this classic soup; this one is simple, wholesome, and filling. Serve with warm, crusty garlic bread.

Heat the olive oil in a large pan and add the garlic. Sauté for about 2 minutes, then stir in the diced carrots and zucchini. Cook for about 5 minutes, stirring occasionally.

Stir in the pastina and chopped parsley into the vegetable mixture, add the vegetable paste and vegetable stock, and season with salt and ground black pepper.

Cover and simmer for about 30 minutes, until the vegetables and pasta have softened and the flavors have developed. Serve with freshly shredded Parmesan cheese.

INGREDIENTS

1 Tbsp extra virgin olive oil
3 garlic cloves, crushed
450 g/1 lb carrots, peeled and diced fine
450 g/1 lb zucchini, diced fine
75 g/3 oz dried pastina (any tiny pasta shapes)
5 Tbsp chopped fresh parsley
50 g/2 oz vegetable paste
6 cups/1.8 l/3 pt well-flavored vegetable stock
salt and ground black pepper
freshly shredded Parmesan cheese, to serve

VEGETABLE AND FRESH CILANTRO SOUP

SERVES 4–6

A light, fresh-tasting soup that is ideal either as an appetizer or as a light lunch.

Bring the vegetable stock to a boil in a large pan, and add the pasta with a dash of olive oil. Cook for about 5 minutes, stirring occasionally, then add the sliced carrots.

Cook for 5 minutes, then add the peas and cilantro. Season with salt and freshly ground black pepper and simmer gently for about 10 minutes, stirring occasionally, until the pasta and carrots are tender. Serve the soup with shredded cheese, if wished.

INGREDIENTS

5 cups/1.2 1/2 pt vegetable stock
175 g/6 oz dried pasta (any shape)
a dash of olive oil
2 medium carrots, sliced thin
1 cup/100g/4 oz frozen peas
6 Tbsp chopped fresh cilantro
salt and ground black pepper

INGREDIENTS

16 dried Chinese mushrooms, soaked in hot water for 30 minutes

7 cups/2 1/3½ pt chicken stock (see page 18)

450 g/1 lb dried white radish

275 g/10 oz mung bean sprouts

1 tsp soy sauce

½ tsp sugar

ground black pepper

WHITE RADISH SOUP
SERVES 4–6

This warming, soothing Korean soup is usually served for breakfast.

Remove the mushrooms from the soaking water. Drain and reserve the water.

Remove and discard the stalks from the mushrooms. Thinly slice the caps and put into a large pan with the stock. Bring to a boil and add the white radish. Cover the pan and simmer slowly for about 10 minutes until the white radish is tender.

Add the bean sprouts, return to a boil. Cover again and simmer for 3 to 4 minutes more. Add the soy sauce, sugar, and pepper.

CHESTNUT AND APPLE SOUP

SERVES 4–6

INGREDIENTS

450 g/1 lb shelled, skinned chestnuts

2 Tbsp butter

1 large onion, chopped

2 medium carrots, thinly sliced

2 medium dessert apples, peeled, cored and finely chopped

4 cups/960 ml/1½ pt water

bouquet garni (bay leaf, 2 sage leaves, thyme sprigs and parsley stems)

salt and freshly ground pepper

4 Tbsp light cream, or as needed

sage leaves and chives, for garnishing

This autumnal soup captures the flavors of the harvest—perfect as a starter at Christmas. For a more exotic, spicy soup, replace the sage with a cinnamon stick.

Put the chestnuts in a saucepan, add water to cover and simmer over medium heat until chestnuts are just tender, 12–15 minutes. Remove from the heat and set aside.

Melt the butter in a large heavy saucepan over medium-high heat, add the onion and carrots, and cook until the onion is just softened, about 5 minutes, stirring frequently. Add the apples, water, *bouquet garni* and chestnuts with their cooking liquid. Season with salt and pepper, and bring to a boil. Reduce the heat and simmer until all the vegetables are tender, about 25 minutes. Remove the *bouquet garni*.

Transfer the solids to a blender or a food processor fitted with a metal blade, add some of the liquid and purée until smooth. Return to the saucepan, add the cream and simmer over low heat for a few minutes until heated through. Taste and adjust the seasoning. Ladle into a warm tureen or soup plates. If you like, garnish with sage leaves and chives on the edge of the plates.

PEANUT SOUP

SERVES 4

Melt the butter or margarine in a large pan over low heat. Add the onion, celery, garlic, and thyme. Cook for 5 minutes, stirring all the time, then gradually add the flour and stock, still stirring constantly. Increase the heat, then stir in the peanut butter or peanuts, and cook over medium-low heat for 10 minutes.

Reduce the heat and add the milk, salt, and pepper. Simmer gently for about 15 minutes.

Serve very hot, garnished with the chopped green bell pepper.

INGREDIENTS

25 g/1 oz butter or margarine

1 onion, grated

1 celery stalk, chopped

1 garlic clove, crushed

1 sprig fresh thyme, chopped

1 Tbsp flour

3¾ cups/900 ml/1½ pt chicken stock

½ cup/50 g/2 oz crunchy peanut butter or

2¼ cups/100 g/4 oz coarsely ground peanuts

1 green bell pepper, chopped

YOGURT SOUP

SERVES 4

This is the perfect kind of soup that you can serve to someone who is feeling a little "under the weather."

Heat the butter or margarine in a large saucepan and add the flour. Stirring continuously, brown gently over medium heat until smooth. Mix in the yogurt, and stir thoroughly, then slowly add the chicken stock.

Bring to a boil and add the rice, if using. Season well, cover and simmer gently for about 15 minutes, or until the rice is soft. Garnish with dried mint and paprika, and serve hot with croutons.

INGREDIENTS

1 Tbsp butter or margarine

1 Tbsp flour

generous 1 cup/240 ml/8 floz plain yogurt, strained

4 cups/1 l/1 ½ pt chicken stock

1 Tbsp rice, washed and drained (optional)

salt and ground black pepper

dried mint and paprika, to garnish

croutons, to serve

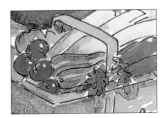

MEDITERRANEAN ROASTED PUMPKIN SOUP

SERVES 4

INGREDIENTS

6 x 1 inch/2.5 cm slices pumpkin, seeded (about 725 g/1 lb 10 oz in total)
6 large tomatoes, halved
1 large onion, sliced thick
4–5 garlic cloves
4 sprigs fresh rosemary
salt and ground black pepper
olive oil
2 cups/500 ml/1 pt water or chicken stock
½ cup/50 g/2 oz pitted black olives, chopped
shavings of fresh Parmesan cheese, to garnish
olive oil bread, to serve

A really raunchy soup to serve before an equally powerful main course! Blend the olives into the soup if you prefer, but they do provide a color and texture contrast in the rich orange broth.

Preheat a 220°C/425°F oven. Arrange all the vegetables in a large roasting pan and tuck the garlic cloves and rosemary in amongst them. Season well, then drizzle with olive oil. Roast for 40 to 50 minutes, until starting to blacken round the edges. The pumpkin should be tender when the other vegetables are ready. Allow the vegetables to cool slightly.

Cut the flesh away from the skin of the pumpkin and chop roughly. Remove the rosemary, then scrape all the vegetables into a blender or food processor, and add the pumpkin flesh. Blend until smooth, then rub the soup through a fine strainer into a pan.

Add the water or stock, then heat the soup slowly until almost at a boil. Season well with salt and pepper, then stir in the chopped olives. Ladle into warmed bowls, garnish with a few shavings of Parmesan, then serve with plenty of olive oil bread for dunking.

TOMATO AND SWEET POTATO SOUP

SERVES 6

Heat the oil and butter or margarine in a large pan. Add the onions, and cook them slowly until they are soft.

Add the sweet potatoes, tomatoes, chicken stock, salt, thyme, orange juice and rind, lemon or lime juice and rind, and freshly ground black pepper to taste. Bring to a boil, then lower the heat, cover the pan, and simmer for about 25 minutes.

Liquidize the soup in a blender, then return it to the pan, and simmer for 5 more minutes to heat it through.

Serve it in warmed soup bowls, garnished with a slice of lemon, orange, and tomato.

INGREDIENTS

I Tbsp oil

I Tbsp butter or margarine

2 onions, chopped fine

225 g/½ lb sweet potatoes, peeled and diced

3 medium tomatoes, skinned and chopped fine

2½ cups/600 ml/I pt chicken stock

I tsp salt

I tsp chopped fresh thyme

juice and shredded rind of I orange

IRISH BARLEY SOUP

SERVES 6

Leeks grew wild in Ireland for many centuries and they are still as much a part of the Irish diet as oats and barley. Combining pearl barley with leeks in this tasty soup makes a very traditional dish.

Cook the leeks in the oil until softened but not browned, then add the spinach, and cook briefly until wilted. Add the barley, stock, and *bouquet garni*, then bring to a boil. Season lightly and add the bay leaves, then cover the pan, and simmer for about 1½ hours, until the barley is tender.

Remove the *bouquet garni* and bay leaves. Season to taste, then stir in the cream, if using, and serve immediately with fresh crusty bread.

INGREDIENTS

300 g/10½ oz leeks, sliced fine

2 Tbsp olive oil

⅔ cup/100 g/4 oz shredded spinach

¼ cup/50 g/2 oz pearl barley

8 cups/2 1/3¼ pt well-flavored chicken or vegetable stock

bouquet garni

salt and ground black pepper

2 bay leaves

¼ cup/60 ml/2 floz heavy cream (optional)

CALLALOO

SERVES 4–6

No matter what its spelling—calaloo, callilu, callau, kalalou, or callaloo—this soup is celebrated throughout the Caribbean. Its name is taken from its chief ingredient, the leaves of the tuberous taro or callaloo plant, but cooks outside the Caribbean have found that fresh spinach, Swiss chard, kale, and Indian bhaji are quite similar to callaloo and a lot easier to track down. Mint-green in color and with a subtle, sharp flavor, the soup makes a refreshing opener for any meal.

Wash and drain the greens, discarding the stems. Chop the leaves into pieces. Place in a large, heavy-based pan with the okra, if using, and the eggplant. Add the water and cook over medium heat until the vegetables are tender, about 15 minutes. (If you have added okra, check frequently as this vegetable tends to become glutinous if overcooked.)

Heat the oil in a heavy frying pan and sauté the onions and garlic until the onions are just translucent. Add the remaining ingredients, plus the onions and garlic, to the vegetables, and simmer for 5 minutes. Purée in a blender or food processor, and serve immediately.

INGREDIENTS

225 g/8 oz fresh spinach, Swiss chard, or Indian bhaji

100 g/4 oz okra, sliced (optional)

225 g/8 oz eggplant, peeled and chopped into bite-sized pieces

4 cups/1 1/1½ pt water

1 Tbsp vegetable oil

2 onions, chopped fine

2 garlic cloves, minced

½ tsp thyme

¼ tsp allspice

2 Tbsp snipped fresh chives

1 fresh chile pepper, seeded and chopped

1 Tbsp white wine vinegar

1 cup/240 ml/8 floz coconut milk

salt and ground black pepper

CREME SAINT-GERMAIN

SERVES 4–6

One of the classic Scandinavian soups Grön Soppa with a mild, delicate flavor, which gets a kick from the horseradish cream.

To make the horseradish cream, simply mix the cream and shredded horseradish together.

For the croutons, mix the flour, cheese, and salt together. Crumble the margarine or butter into the mixture. Add the water and quickly mix the pastry together into a ball. Let the pastry rest in a cool place for 30 minutes.

Meanwhile preheat a 240°C/475°F oven. Roll out the pastry to a thickness of ⅛ inch/ 3mm and cut out croutons. Brush with beaten egg and place on a baking sheet. Bake until golden brown, about 5 to 8 minutes.

Fry the onion in 1 tablespoon of the butter or margarine, without browning. Pour in the stock and add the peas. Boil the mixture for 15 minutes. Blend in a food processor, then strain.

Melt the rest of the butter or margarine and stir in the flour. Cook for 2 to 3 minutes, stirring. Gradually add the strained soup and stir in the brandy or wine and season to taste.

Whisk the egg yolk and cream in a soup tureen and pour in the soup, stirring vigorously. Serve the soup in warmed bowls garnished with horseradish cream and cheese croutons.

INGREDIENTS

1 medium onion, sliced

2 Tbsp butter or margarine

4¼ cups/1 l/1½ pt veal or chicken stock

300 g/11 oz fresh shelled peas, or 1 small packet frozen peas

1 Tbsp flour

1–2 Tbsp brandy or Madeira

salt and ground black pepper

1 egg yolk

⅓ cup/80 ml/3 floz light cream

Horseradish cream

⅔ cup/160 ml/5 floz heavy cream

2–2½ tsp shredded horseradish

Cheese croutons

1¾ cups/250 g/9 oz flour

100 g/4 oz Swiss cheese, shredded

a pinch of salt

25 g/1 oz butter or margarine

2 Tbsp ice water

1 egg, to glaze

CHAPTER TWO

COLD VEGETABLES

APPETIZING AND NUTRITIOUS
VEGETABLE SOUPS THAT
WILL BE ENJOYED ON EVEN
THE HOTTEST OF
SUMMER DAYS.

INGREDIENTS

½ medium red cabbage, cored and chopped
coarse

1 Tbsp vegetable oil

1 large onion, chopped

1 large leek, split and sliced

1 large carrot, sliced thin

1 medium parsnip, sliced thin

⅔ cup/160 ml/5 floz red wine

5 cups/1.2 1/2 pt chicken stock or water, plus
more if needed

6 medium beets, peeled and cubed

4 tomatoes, peeled, seeded, and
chopped coarse

bay leaf

1 tsp sherry vinegar or red wine vinegar

sour cream or yogurt

chopped fresh dill, to garnish

COLD BORSCHT
SERVES 6

There is no single definitive recipe for Borscht, the popular Eastern European peasant soup. In fact, there seem to be almost limitless variations—some with meat, some with beans, some mainly cabbage, others mainly beets. This meatless version offers a balanced combination of vegetable flavors that meld when chilled.

Cover the cabbage with cold water. Set over high heat, bring to a boil, and boil for 3 minutes. Drain.

Heat the oil in a large pan over medium-low heat and add the onion and leek. Cover and sweat the vegetables until soft, about 5 minutes, stirring occasionally. Add the carrot, parsnip, blanched cabbage, and wine. Bring to a boil and add the stock or water, beets, tomatoes, and bay leaf. Bring back to a boil, reduce the heat, and simmer until all the vegetables are just tender, about 1¼ hours.

Remove the bay leaf and, using a slotted spoon, transfer the solids to a blender or food processor fitted with a steel blade, working in batches if necessary. Add some of the cooking liquid and purée until smooth.

Strain the purée and any remaining cooking liquid into a large bowl. Stir in the vinegar, leave to cool, and chill until cold. If you wish, thin the soup with water or more stock.

Season to taste with salt and pepper, and add a little more vinegar, if liked. Ladle into chilled soup bowls or plates, top each with a dollop of sour cream or yogurt and sprinkle with dill.

INGREDIENTS

2 Hungarian cherry peppers (or red
bell peppers)
2 Tbsp sunflower oil
1 onion, chopped fine
1 garlic clove, minced
2½ cups/600 ml/1 pt vegetable or chicken
stock
225 g/8 oz ripe tomatoes, peeled and
seeded
salt and ground black pepper
2 Tbsp light cream, and chopped Hungarian
cherry pepper, to serve

HUNGARIAN CHERRY PEPPER SOUP

SERVES 4

Preheat the broiler. Rinse the peppers and cut in half, discarding the seeds. Place, skin-side up, on a sheet of aluminum foil in a broiler pan under the broiler. Drizzle with 1 tablespoon of the oil and broil for 5 to 10 minutes, or until the skins have blistered. Remove from the heat and leave to cool. When cool, remove the skins and roughly chop.

Meanwhile, heat the remaining oil in a pan and sauté the onion and garlic for 5 minutes, or until transparent but not browned. Add the chopped peppers and then the stock. Roughly chop the tomatoes and add to the pan with seasoning to taste. Bring to a boil, then cover, and simmer gently for 15 minutes, or until the peppers are soft.

Leave to cool, then purée in a food processor or strainer. Chill for 1 hour.

To serve, add the cream and swirl lightly, then sprinkle with a little chopped cherry pepper.

INGREDIENTS

1 Tbsp butter

4 shallots, chopped fine

6 cups shelled fresh peas or thawed
frozen peas

4 cups/1 1/1½ pt water

salt and ground black pepper

⅔ cup/160 ml/5 floz heavy cream

2 Tbsp chopped fresh mint

12–18 small snow peas, blanched and chilled,
to garnish

CHILLED GREEN PEA SOUP

SERVES 6

This soup is a stunning bright green color. It is simple to make and quite tasty using frozen peas, but if you are able to find fresh-picked young garden peas, you are in for a real gourmet treat.

Melt the butter in a large pan over medium-low heat. Add the shallots and cook, stirring occasionally, until they begin to soften, about 5 minutes.

Add the peas and water. Season with salt and a little pepper. Simmer, covered, stirring occasionally, until the vegetables are tender, about 12 minutes for frozen or young fresh peas, or up to 18 minutes for large peas.

Transfer the solids to a blender or a food processor fitted with a steel blade. Add some of the cooking liquid and purée until smooth, working in batches if necessary. Strain into a bowl with the remaining cooking liquid, allow to stand until cool, cover, and chill until cold.

Using an electric mixer or whisk, whip the cream in a chilled bowl until soft peaks form. Stir in the mint.

Thin the soup with a little cold water, if needed, and adjust the seasoning. Ladle into chilled soup plates and garnish with a dollop of cream and 2 or 3 snow peas.

COOK'S TIP
You will need 2.25-2.75 kg/5–6 lb of fresh peas in the pod to obtain 6 cups of shelled peas.

TOMATO AND CILANTRO SOUP

SERVES 6

INGREDIENTS

1.5 kg/3 lb ripe, plump tomatoes, roughly chopped

¾ cup/180 ml/6 floz tomato juice

3 Tbsp freshly squeezed orange juice

1 Greek or Italian pickled pepper, seeded

¾ tsp superfine sugar

ice water

4 Tbsp fresh cilantro, chopped fine

⅔ cup/150 ml/¼ pt Greek-style yogurt

This summer soup makes the most of a glut of plump, juicy tomatoes. The piquant flavor of cilantro offsets them wonderfully. This would make an ideal appetizer to be served before a fish or poultry main dish.

In a blender or food processor fitted with a metal blade, purée the tomatoes, tomato and orange juices, pepper, and sugar until as smooth as possible. Press the purée through a strainer, rubbing with a wooden spoon to force as much through as possible.

Discard the residue, and add enough ice water to thin the purée to a soup-like consistency. Stir in the cilantro, cover, and chill until cold. Pass around the yogurt separately at the table, to allow guests to add as much of it as they wish.

CHILLED CUCUMBER AND GREEN CHILE SOUP

SERVES 6

INGREDIENTS

4 large scallions, trimmed and sliced

1 lemon grass stalk, bruised and chopped fine

1–2 garlic cloves, crushed

2 each green and caribe chiles, seeded and chopped fine, or 3 green chiles

2 lime leaves, shredded fine

1 vegetable stock cube, crumbled

4 cups/1 1/1½ pt water

1 large cucumber, weighing about 450 g/1 lb, seeded and chopped

1 cup/240 ml/8 floz plain yogurt

1 tbsp fish sauce

salt

2 Tbsp chopped fresh cilantro

This soup is highly spiced which counteracts the "flavor numbing" effect of chilling.

Place the scallions, lemon grass, garlic, chiles, and lime leaves in a pan with the stock cube. Pour in the water, then bring to a boil. Add the cucumber, cover the pan, remove from heat, and leave to marinate for 1 hour.

Purée the soup in a blender or food processor until smooth, then press the mixture through a fine strainer with the back of a ladle. Whisk in the yogurt and fish sauce, then season the soup to taste with a little salt if necessary. Chill very well, for at least 2 hours.

Add the cilantro to the soup just before serving, and spoon the soup over about a tablespoon of crushed ice in each individual bowl.

INGREDIENTS

3½ cups/840 ml/28 floz vegetable stock

1 onion, chopped

1 garlic clove, minced

3 zucchini, shredded

1 large potato, scrubbed and chopped

1 Tbsp chopped fresh mint

ground black pepper

⅔ cup/160 ml/5 floz low-fat plain yogurt

mint sprigs and zucchini strips, to garnish

ZUCCHINI AND MINT SOUP

SERVES 4

This delicate soup has a silky texture and a hint of mint.

Put half of the vegetable stock in a large pan, add the onion and garlic, and cook for 5 minutes over a gentle heat until the onion softens. Add the shredded zucchini, potato, and the remaining stock. Stir in the mint and cook over gentle heat for 20 minutes or until the potato is cooked.

Transfer the soup to a food processor and blend for 10 seconds, until almost smooth. Turn the soup into a bowl, season, and stir in the yogurt. Cover and chill for 2 hours. Spoon the soup into individual serving bowls or a soup tureen, garnish, and serve.

COLD AVOCADO SOUP

SERVES 4–6

Preheat the broiler to high. Cut the chiles in half and discard the seeds. Place in a broiler pan, skin-side uppermost, and drizzle with the oil. Broil for 5 minutes, or until the skin has blistered. Remove from the heat and leave to cool.

Discard the skin and membrane from the chiles and roughly chop. Put into a food processor. Peel and seed the avocados, then roughly chop, and put into the processor with the stock. Blend to form a smooth purée.

With the machine still running at low speed, add the cream, then add the milk slowly.

Stir in the lime juice and seasoning to taste. Pour into a soup tureen and chill for at least 1 hour. Serve garnished with snipped chives and sour cream.

INGREDIENTS

1 or 2 green Anaheim chiles

1 Tbsp oil

3 large ripe avocados

⅔ cup/160 ml/5 floz chicken or vegetable stock

1¼ cups/300 ml/½ pt light cream

⅔ cup/160 ml/5 floz milk

1 to 2 Tbsp lime juice

salt and white pepper

snipped fresh chives and sour cream, to garnish

INGREDIENTS

3 garlic cloves

4 thick slices Greek bread or baguette,
crusts removed

15 g/½ oz stick butter

2 red onions, sliced thin

8 radishes, sliced thin

7 large ripe tomatoes, skinned, seeded,
and chopped

½ cucumber, peeled and sliced thin

salt and ground black pepper

a large dash of Tabasco

5 Tbsp vegetable oil

1 Tbsp lemon juice

400 g/14 oz can chicken consommé

⅔ cup/160 ml/5 floz Greek-style yogurt

8 scallions, chopped fine

CHILLED VEGETABLE SOUP
SERVES 4–6

This is an extraordinarily refreshing soup—like a liquid salad. Based on ingredients found all over the Central Republics of Russia, it is a refined variation on a common theme.

Finely chop two of the garlic cloves and set aside. Halve and use the remaining clove to rub over the bread slices. Roughly cut them into croutons.

Heat the butter in a frying pan and sauté the croutons until golden. Drain and set aside.

In a large bowl, combine the chopped garlic, red onions, radishes, tomatoes, cucumber, seasoning to taste, and the Tabasco. In a small bowl, whisk together the oil and lemon juice, then pour over the salad and chill for about 1 hour.

Place the chicken consommé in the refrigerator 30 minutes before you make the soup. Just before serving, add the chilled consommé to the bowl and stir it in thoroughly, then stir in the yogurt. Sprinkle with the scallions, and serve the croutons in a separate bowl.

CHAPTER THREE

BEANS AND PULSES

HEALTHY, DELICIOUS SOUP
RECIPES THAT CAN BE SERVED
AS EITHER APPETIZERS OR AS
MAIN MEALS IN THEIR
OWN RIGHT.

SPICY BLACK BEAN SOUP

SERVES 4–6

This soup has its roots in Cuba, but it shows the influence of contemporary chefs and the excitement of the food scene in Florida today.

Pick over the beans to remove any small stones. Cover with cold water and leave to soak for 6 hours or overnight.

Drain the beans, put into a saucepan with cold water to cover and set over high heat. Bring to a boil and boil for 10 minutes. Drain and rinse well.

Heat the oil in a large, heavy saucepan over medium-high heat, add the onions and cook until they are just softened, 3–4 minutes, stirring frequently. Add the garlic and continue cooking for 2 minutes. Add the brandy, water, *bouquet garni*, cumin seeds, oregano and chilies. When the mixture begins to bubble, stir in the tomato paste, reduce the heat to low and simmer gently, partially covered, for 1½–2½ hours until the beans are tender, stirring occasionally. Remove and discard the *bouquet garni* and season with salt and, if you wish, pepper.

Ladle the soup into a warm tureen or bowls and top with a dollop of sour cream. Sprinkle with the scallions and garnish with cilantro.

INGREDIENTS

2½ cups/200 g/8 oz black beans

1 Tbsp olive oil

2 red onions, finely chopped

4 garlic cloves, minced

5 Tbsp brandy

8 cups/2 1/3½ pt water

bouquet garni (bay leaf, thyme and marjoram sprigs, cilantro and parsley stems and 2–3 strips orange zest)

½ tsp cumin seeds

¼ tsp dried oregano

3–4 roasted ancho chile peppers, seeded and chopped, or ¼ tsp crushed dried chilies

1 Tbsp tomato paste

3 tomatoes, peeled, seeded and chopped

salt and freshly ground pepper

6 Tbsp sour cream

3–4 scallions, finely chopped

cilantro leaves, for garnishing

GALICIAN BEAN, PORK, AND GREENS SOUP

SERVES 6

This is a traditional springtime soup from Galicia in Spain. The flavor comes from salt meat: use fresh spareribs or salt pork, whichever is easiest.

If using pork spareribs, rub them well with salt. Alternatively, salt pork must be blanched. Put it with the ham knuckle bone in a pan, cover with cold water, and bring to a boil. Simmer for 5 minutes then drain. Cube the pork.

Drain the beans and put them, with the meat and bones, into a casserole. Add 4¼ pints/2.7 l water, bring to a simmer, skim off any scum, then cook gently, covered, for 1 hour.

Add the potatoes and simmer until done (about 20 minutes). Remove all the bones from the pot and taste the stock. Season with salt and pepper as necessary. Add the greens and simmer for 5 to 10 minutes. Return all the meat from the bones to the pan. To thicken the liquid a little, mash in a few potatoes.

INGREDIENTS

350 g/¾ lb pork spareribs or 100 g/4 oz salt pork

salt

450 g/1 lb smoked ham knuckle bone with meat

1¼ cups/150 g/6 oz dried navy beans, soaked overnight

450 g/1 lb new potatoes

ground black pepper

200 g/7 oz tender turnip leaves or kale

INGREDIENTS

2 Tbsp olive oil

3 garlic cloves, minced

4 Tbsp chopped fresh parsley

150 g/5 oz dried whole-wheat gnocchi
piccoli (shells)

7½ pt/1.8 l/3 pt vegetable stock

3 Tbsp vegetable or tomato paste

375 g/14 oz can mixed beans, such as
borlotti, kidney, cannellini, etc, drained

salt and ground black pepper

freshly shredded Parmesan cheese, to serve

PASTA BEAN SOUP

SERVES 4–6

A nutritious meal in itself—low-fat and full of protein. Serve with warm, crusty garlic bread.

Heat the oil in a large pan, and sauté the garlic with the chopped parsley for about 2 minutes. Add the gnocchi piccoli and cook for 1 to 2 minutes, stirring constantly.

Pour in the vegetable stock, and add the vegetable or tomato paste. Bring to a boil, reduce the heat, then simmer for about 10 minutes, stirring occasionally, until the pasta is tender.

Add the beans, and season with salt and freshly ground black pepper. Continue to cook for a further 5 minutes, then serve with a little freshly shredded Parmesan cheese.

CABBAGE, BEAN, AND HAM SOUP

SERVES 6

INGREDIENTS

1 cup/100 g/4 oz dried lima beans

1 Tbsp olive oil

1 cup/100 g/4 oz chopped onion

3 garlic cloves, minced

2 carrots, peeled and chopped

7½ pt/1.8 l/3 pt chicken stock

2 cups/500 ml/1 pt water

2 cups/200 g/8 oz diced ham

2 sprigs of parsley

2 bay leaves

1 tsp fresh thyme or ¼ tsp dried

¼ tsp dried sage

3 cups/200 g/8 oz shredded green cabbage

salt and ground black pepper

Serve this hearty winter soup with cornmeal bread and cheese.

Put the lima beans in a large pan. Add 1 quart of water. Bring the water to a boil, for 2 minutes. Remove the pan from the heat, and let the beans soak for 1 hour in the hot water. Drain the beans.

In a small frying pan, sauté the onion, garlic and carrots in olive oil for 5 minutes. Put the beans and the vegetables in the large pan with the chicken stock, 2 cups water, ham, parsley, bay leaves, thyme, and sage. Simmer, uncovered, until the beans are tender, about 1 hour. Add the cabbage. Cook until the cabbage is tender, 5 minutes. Add salt and pepper to taste.

LENTIL SOUP

SERVES 6 – 8

INGREDIENTS

¾ cup/100 g/4 oz green lentils

2 Tbsp olive oil

1 red onion, chopped fine

2 garlic cloves, chopped

350 g/12 oz shin of veal, chopped

½ tsp each ground cumin and cinnamon

¼ tsp cayenne pepper

generous 7½ pt/1.8 l/3 pt water

3 small-to-medium carrots, diced

3 celery stalks

2 potatoes, diced

salt and ground black pepper

1 bunch of cilantro, chopped coarse

lemon juice

Lentils have, for many years, provided a simple, adaptable, accessible, and portable source of protein and calories. This version has a middle-Eastern flavor.

Boil the lentils in a pan of water for at least 10 minutes, drain, and set aside. Heat the oil in a pan, then cook the onion, garlic, and veal, stirring frequently, until the onion is soft. Stir in the spices until fragrant, then add the lentils and water. Bring to a boil and skim the scum from the surface. Partly cover and simmer for about 1 hour until the meat is tender.

Add the vegetables and cook for a further 30 to 40 minutes. Season and stir in the cilantro and lemon juice to taste. Serve straight away.

GARBANZO WITH SPINACH

SERVES 6

This soup-stew is made with, or without, salt cod. The latter makes a pleasant vegetarian dish.

Remove the bones and skin from the salt cod (if using) and shred the flesh. Put the drained garbanzos, salt cod, 1 whole onion stick with a clove, whole carrot, bay leaf, and parsley stalks into a large casserole and add 5 cups water. Bring slowly to a simmer, skim off the bubbles, then cover and simmer for 1½ to 2 hours.

Heat the oil in a shallow frying pan and fry the chopped onion. As it softens add the garlic, tomatoes, and paprika. Cook down to a sauce, seasoning with salt and pepper.

Add the spinach to a panful of boiling water—just in and out for young spinach, but cook older leaves for 2 to 3 minutes.

Drain and chop.

When the garbanzos are almost tender, remove the bay leaf, parsley stalks, whole onion, and carrot. Discard the clove and purée the onion and carrot in a blender or food processor with 3 tablespoons of the garbanzos and half a ladleful of their liquid. Check the amount of liquid: the garbanzos should be barely covered at this point. Pour off some water if necessary.

Add the tomato sauce and onion purée to the casserole. Taste for seasoning—plenty is needed. Add the spinach, simmer for another 20 minutes or so to blend the flavors, then check that the garbanzos are tender. Traditionally the soup is served with chopped hard-cooked egg on top.

INGREDIENTS

200 g/7 oz salt cod, soaked overnight (optional)

1⅔ cup/175 g/6 oz garbanzo beans, soaked overnight

2 onions, 1 whole, peeled, 1 chopped

1 clove

1 large carrot

1 bay leaf

2–3 parsley stalks, bruised

3 Tbsp olive oil

2 garlic cloves, chopped fine

2 ripe tomatoes, skinned and chopped

1 tsp paprika

salt and ground black pepper

800 g/1¾ lb spinach, trimmed and washed

2 hard-cooked eggs, peeled and chopped

ASTURIAN BEAN AND SAUSAGE POT

SERVES 6

Fabada Asturiana *is one of the world's most famous bean pots. It is flavored with cured sausages, to give an incredible richness to the flat, white lima beans.*

Choose a stockpot that holds at least 30 cups/7.5 l/12½ pints. Cover the beans, in a bowl, with plenty of boiling water. Put the salt meat (salt pork and ham bone) into the pot and cover with cold water. Bring to a boil, then drain the meat, and return to the stockpot.

Drain the beans then add to the pot with the peppercorns, paprika, saffron, and bay leaf. Add 12 cups/3 l/4¾ pints water. Bring slowly to a boil, then simmer very gently on minimum heat for 2 hours. A big pot on a small burner is best, and better still with a heat diffuser. Check occasionally that the beans are still covered, but do not stir (or they will break up).

Remove the ham bone and salt pork, to cool a little. Strip off the skin and fat, and take about 2 tablespoons of chopped fat for frying (or use oil). Sweat this in a shallow skillet. In the fat it makes, fry the garlic lightly, then spoon it into the beans.

Fry the sliced sausages and morcilla or blood sausage (discarding any artificial casings). Stir into the pot with the pan fat.

Remove all the meat from the ham bone. Chop it, and the salt pork or beef, and return to the pot; simmer over a medium heat for a few minutes. Check the seasonings (there should be enough salt from the meat). Serve with fresh greens.

INGREDIENTS

725g/1 lb 10 oz dried lima beans

675 g/1½ lb salt pork

675 g/1½ lb smoked ham knuckle or back, skin slashed

6 black peppercorns, crushed

1 tsp paprika

a pinch of powdered saffron

1 bay leaf

2 Tbsp oil (optional)

4 garlic cloves, chopped

450 g/1 lb chorizos or smoked sausages, like kabanos

175 g/6 oz morcilla or blood sausage

INGREDIENTS

4 large onions, sliced fine

3 garlic cloves, sliced fine

2 Tbsp vegetable oil

I Tbsp butter

I red chile, seeded and chopped fine

I tsp mild chili powder

½ tsp ground turmeric

I tsp ground cilantro

salt and ground black pepper

10½ cups/2.5 I/4¼ pt vegetable or chicken stock

50 g/8 oz/¼ cup couscous

chopped fresh cilantro, to garnish

LEBANESE COUSCOUS SOUP

SERVES 6

Couscous, tiny grains made from semolina, is usually steamed over a stew or stock. In this recipe, the couscous is used to thicken a richly spiced onion soup.

Cook the onions and garlic in the oil and melted butter until well browned. This will take about 15 minutes over medium high heat. You must let the onions brown to achieve a rich color for the finished soup.

Stir in the chopped chile and the spices and cook over low heat for a further 1 to 2 minutes before adding the stock. Cover and simmer gently for 30 minutes.

Stir the couscous into the soup, return to a boil, and simmer for a further 10 minutes. Season to taste, then garnish with the cilantro and serve immediately.

CHAPTER FOUR

SEAFOOD

A TRULY INTERNATIONAL
SELECTION OF RECIPES
FEATURING A VARIETY
OF FISH AND SHELLFISH
SOUPS TO SUIT
ALL TASTES.

OYSTER STEW

SERVES 4

Essentially oysters cooked in cream, this rich 'stew' is deceptively easy.

In a medium pan over low heat, melt the butter. Sautée the scallions and celery until limp, about 5 minutes.

Add the light cream, salt, cayenne and Worcestershire sauce and heat until the soup just starts to boil. Lower the heat, add the oysters and their liquor and cook just until the edges of the oysters start to curl, 2 to 3 minutes. Taste and adjust the seasonings.

Garnish each bowl with a pat of butter or a dash of sherry.

INGREDIENTS

25 g/1 oz butter

4 scallions, finely chopped

25 g/1 oz celery, finely chopped

5 cups/1.2 1/2 pt light cream

½ tsp salt

¼ tsp cayenne pepper

2 tsp Worcestershire sauce

3 dozen large or 4 dozen small-medium oysters with their liquor, large oysters halved

butter or sherry, to garnish

HOT AND SOUR NOODLE SOUP WITH SHRIMP

SERVES 4

This is one of the representative dishes of Thai cuisine. The broth is a myriad of flavors: the sour element of lime leaves and lemon grass combined with the hot chile pepper and fish sauce, with its strong seafood aroma.

Heat the oil in a pan, then stir-fry the garlic, shallots, galangal or ginger, and chile for about 1 minute. Add the chicken stock, lime leaves, and lemon grass, bring to a boil, and simmer for 5 minutes.

Meanwhile, soak the rice vermicelli for 3 minutes, rinse, drain, and divide into four bowls. Add the shrimp, fish sauce, lemon or lime juice, sugar, and straw mushrooms to the soup, then simmer for 2 to 3 minutes.

Pour the soup into the bowls and sprinkle with the cilantro leaves. Serve immediately whilst piping hot.

INGREDIENTS

1 Tbsp vegetable oil

2 garlic cloves, minced

2 shallots, shredded

1 inch/2.5 cm piece galangal, or ½-inch/1 cm piece fresh ginger root, sliced thin

4–5 small red chiles, chopped

6 cups/1.5 1/2½ pt light chicken stock (see page 18)

3 kafir lime leaves, sliced

4 inch/10 cm piece lemon grass, chopped

225 g/½ lb rice vermicelli

20 peeled tiger shrimp

6 Tbsp fish sauce

6 Tbsp fresh lemon or lime juice

2 Tbsp brown sugar

16 canned straw mushrooms

cilantro leaves

SQUID WITH BELL PEPPERS AND TOMATO

SERVES 4

Cook the squid gently so that it is not irrevocably toughened.

Cut the squid open into two halves; then cut across into 1 inch/2.5 cm slices.

Heat the oil in a flameproof casserole. Add the onions, garlic, and bell peppers, and cook until softened. Stir in the tomatoes and bubble until well-blended and lightly thickened. Add the stock and wine, bring to a boil, and then lower the heat. Add the squid and seasoning, cover, and cook gently for 1 to 1½ hours, or until the squid is tender and the cooking juices have reduced to a light sauce; if necessary, remove the lid towards the end of cooking to allow the sauce to evaporate slightly.

Toast the bread, cut the slices in half, and put into a warmed, deep serving dish. Pour over the squid mixture and sprinkle with parsley, and serve immediately.

INGREDIENTS

1 kg/2¼ lb prepared squid

½ cup/120 ml/4 floz olive oil

2 onions, chopped fine

1 garlic clove, crushed

2 red bell peppers, cored, seeded, and sliced

450 g/1 lb well-flavored tomatoes, chopped

1 cup/240 ml/8 floz fish stock

6 Tbsp dry white wine

salt and ground black pepper

CLAM AND ZUCCHINI SOUP
SERVES 4

The recipe for this delicious soup comes from the Portuguese coast.

Put the clams into a large pan, cover, and heat gently until the shells open. Reserve the juice and shell half the clams; reserve the other half for garnish.

Fry the garlic in the oil until softened and lightly colored; do not allow it to darken. Stir in the zucchini, lemon rind, and cilantro; then add the stock or water. Bring to a boil, cover, and simmer for 10 to 15 minutes until the zucchini are very tender.

Purée the soup in a blender or food processor, or pass through a food mill. Return to the pan and add the opened clams and reserved juice. Reheat gently without allowing the soup to boil as this would toughen the clams. Add the lemon juice and seasoning to taste.

To serve, rub the toasted bread with the garlic and place a slice in each of four warmed soup bowls. Pour over the soup, sprinkle with olive oil, and serve.

INGREDIENTS

675 g/1½ lb baby clams, cleaned
1 plump garlic clove, chopped fine
3 Tbsp olive oil
675 g/1½ lb zucchini, sliced thick
finely shredded rind of 1 small lemon, plus a squeeze of juice
1 Tbsp chopped fresh cilantro
4¼ cups/1 1/1¾ pt fish or vegetable stock or water
salt and ground black pepper

To serve

4 thick slices country bread, toasted
1 plump garlic clove, lightly crushed
olive oil

SQUID, PUMPKIN, AND TOMATO SOUP

SERVES 4

Squid should be cooked very briefly to avoid it becoming chewy.

Cook the onion for 5 to 6 minutes in the oil in a large pan over low heat, until softened but not browned. Add the pumpkin, continue to cook for 3 to 4 minutes, then stir in the squid. Increase the heat and cook for 2 to 3 minutes, until the squid is opaque, then add the garlic and paprika. Lower the heat and continue cooking for a further 2 to 3 minutes.

Add the puréed tomatoes or tomato juice, the stock, and bay leaves. Season well, then bring the soup slowly to a boil. Cover, and cook over very low heat for 1½ to 2 hours, stirring occasionally.

Remove the bay leaves, then adjust the seasoning if necessary. Add a little water if the soup has become too thick.

Serve in warmed bowls with a swirl of cream and a scattering of freshly chopped parsley.

INGREDIENTS

1 large onion, chopped fine

3 Tbsp extra virgin olive oil

3 cups/200 g/8 oz peeled, seeded, and diced pumpkin

450 g/1 lb prepared squid rings

2 garlic cloves, sliced fine

2 tsp paprika

2 cups/500 ml/1 pt puréed tomatoes or thick tomato juice

1 cup/240 ml/8 floz fish or vegetable stock

2 bay leaves

salt and ground black pepper

light cream and chopped fresh parsley, to garnish

OYSTERS IN PARSLEY AND GARLIC CREAM

SERVES 4

INGREDIENTS

16–20 fresh oysters

1 large bunch of curly-leaf parsley, stems removed (about 6 cups leaves)

1½ cups/360 ml/12 floz heavy cream

1–2 garlic cloves, chopped fine

3–4 Tbsp shellfish stock or water (optional)

salt and ground black pepper

1 ripe tomato (preferably plum), peeled, seeded, and diced

The parsley in this creamy soup tames the garlic and gives it a brilliant color. It is delicious made with plump succulent oysters, but if you prefer, you can substitute cooked mussels or snails.

Working over a bowl to catch the juices, open the oysters: hold in a cloth (flat-side up), push the knife into the hinge, then work it around until you can pry off the top shell. When all the oysters have been opened, strain the liquid through a strainer lined with damp cheesecloth. Remove the oysters to the filtered liquid. (This may be done several hours in advance; chill, covered.)

Bring a large pan of salted water to a boil. Drop in the parsley leaves and cook for 3 to 4 minutes until bright green and tender. Drain and refresh in cold water. Press with the back of a spoon to extract as much water as possible. (This may be done up to 1 day in advance.)

Combine the cream and garlic in a medium pan and simmer over medium-low heat for 15 minutes until the garlic is tender and the cream has thickened slightly. Transfer to a blender or a food processor fitted with a steel blade, add the parsley, and purée until smooth. Return the purée to the pan and stir in the oyster liquid. If you wish, thin with shellfish stock or water.

Season to taste with salt, if needed, and pepper. Simmer the soup gently for about 5 minutes. Add the oysters and continue cooking for 1 to 2 minutes until the oysters are just heated through. Remove them with a slotted spoon and divide among four warm shallow soup plates. Ladle over the soup and garnish with diced tomato.

LEEK AND MUSSEL SOUP

SERVES 4

INGREDIENTS

12½ cups/3 1/5 pt fresh mussels

4 leeks

2 shallots

2 garlic cloves

3 Tbsp chopped fresh parsley

1 Tbsp chopped fresh dill

1 Tbsp snipped fresh chives

Half bottle dry white wine

1 stick butter, cut into small cubes

5 cups/1.2 1/2 pt fish stock

a small pinch of saffron soaked in water

ground black pepper

Prepare the mussels by removing the beards and any barnacles. Scrub well and rinse in clean water. Throw away any mussels that are broken or remain open when tapped. Place in a pan.

Chop the leeks, shallots, and garlic finely. Put in a pan with the parsley, dill, and chives.

Pour the wine over the clean mussels. Place on high heat until the mussels are steamed open. Discard any mussels that remain firmly closed. Take out the mussels, shell, and reserve. Reserve the liquor. Whip the butter cubes into the liquor.

Add the fish stock to the pan. Stir in the soaked saffron strands, simmer gently over low heat for a few minutes, and season with black pepper.

Add the shelled mussels and heat in the liquor but do not boil, as the mussels will get leathery.

Serve the soup in warm bowls garnished with more snipped chives and parsley. Serve with warm bread.

INGREDIENTS

1 red bell pepper, diced

1½ Tbsp chopped scallions, including a small amount of green tops

2 cups/500 ml/¾ pt homemade chicken stock or canned, with fat strained out

2 tsp chopped garlic

1 Tbsp grated fresh ginger root

1 Tbsp ground cilantro

½ Tbsp curry powder

½ tsp dried thyme

½ tsp white pepper

½ tsp hot pepper sauce

1¾ cups/420 ml/14 floz coconut milk

550 g/1¼ lb medium shrimp, shelled and deveined

1 cup/240 ml/8 floz heavy cream

COCONUT SHRIMP SOUP

SERVES 4

In a small bowl, mix together the red bell pepper and chopped scallions, and set aside.

In a 4-quart Dutch oven or pan over medium-high heat, bring the chicken stock, garlic, ginger, cilantro, curry powder, thyme, pepper, hot pepper sauce, and coconut milk to a boil. Reduce the heat immediately and simmer for 5 minutes. Remove from the heat and skim any fat off the top.

Return to medium-high heat, bring to a simmer, and add half the red bell pepper and scallion mixture, and the shrimp. Simmer just until the shrimp is done, about 5 minutes. Do not overcook.

Remove from the heat and stir in the cream. Taste and adjust the seasoning. Ladle into warmed bowls, and garnish with the remaining red bell pepper and scallion mixture. Serve immediately with warm fresh bread.

RAMEN WITH CRAB OMELET

SERVES 4

Typically, crab omelet is served on its own. The inspiration behind the dish is Chinese, but the Japanese have a preference for it served on a bowl of noodles.

First, to make the omelet, put the eggs, crab meat, mushrooms, scallion, and bamboo shoots in a bowl. Season with salt and pepper, and mix.

Heat the oil in a frying pan or wok until very hot. Pour in the egg mixture, and heat for 30 seconds. Stir lightly with chopsticks or a spatula a few times. When it is nearly set, turn it over. The mixture should be soft like scrambled eggs, but be cooked just enough to be able to retain the shape of an omelet.

Boil plenty of water in a large pan. Add the noodles and cook over a high heat for 3 minutes, or according to the instructions on the package. Drain, then divide among four bowls.

Heat the soy sauce broth. Place the crab meat on the noodles and pour the broth over the top. Sprinkle with the chopped scallion and serve.

INGREDIENTS

450 g/1 lb ramen noodles, or 375 g/14 oz fresh or 350 g/¾ lb dried thin egg noodles

6 cups/1.5 l/2½ pt soy sauce broth (see page 18)

Omelet

6 eggs

175 g/6 oz canned crab meat

4 shiitake mushrooms, sliced

2 scallions, sliced thin

4 Tbsp canned bamboo shoots, sliced thin

salt and white pepper

2–3 Tbsp vegetable oil

1 chopped scallion, to garnish

CATALAN MUSSEL SOUP

SERVES 4

This is one of the best Spanish mussel soups, which has a hint of anis, though a big glass of dry white wine can replace the spirits.

Clean the mussels. Cover them with cold water then scrub them one by one. Pull off all the "beards." Throw out any that are broken or do not close when tapped.

Meanwhile, heat the oil in a pan large enough to contain all the ingredients and fry the onion gently, adding the garlic when it softens. Add the chopped tomato flesh and juice to the pan and cook until reduced to a sauce. Add ⅔ cup water to the pan.

Add the mussels in two or three batches. Cook with the lid on for 3 to 4 minutes until they open. Then use a slotted spoon to remove them to a plate and discard the top shell of each one. Throw away any that remain closed. When they are all done, return them to the pan and sprinkle with the *anis* or Pernod.

Add more water—about 1⅓ cups, and bring back to simmering. Season with salt and pepper, adding cayenne pepper, lemon juice to taste, and parsley. Break a slice of bread into the bottom of each bowl and ladle in the soup.

INGREDIENTS

900 g/2 lb fresh mussels

2 Tbsp olive oil

I mild Spanish onion, chopped

I garlic clove, chopped fine

2 large, ripe tomatoes, skinned, seeded, and chopped

½ cup/120 ml/6 floz anis, *aguadiente* (or Pernod)

salt and ground black pepper

a pinch of cayenne pepper

juice of ½ lemon

2 Tbsp chopped fresh parsley

4 slices of stale bread

INGREDIENTS

3 Tbsp butter

10–12 celery stalks, chopped

1 onion, chopped

¼ tsp dried thyme

½ tsp red pepper flakes

1 Tbsp fresh lemon zest

3 Tbsp self-rising flour

1⅓ cups/360 ml/12 floz chicken stock

1⅓ cups/360 ml/12 floz milk

450 g/1 lb lobster meat or substitute

2 Tbsp dry sherry

salt and ground white pepper

1 Tbsp sweet red bell pepper slivers, to garnish

a pinch paprika, to garnish

SHERRIED LOBSTER BISQUE

SERVES 4–6

This is a rich, delectable soup. Use angler-fish, commonly called monkfish, if you can, because it tastes like the more expensive lobster when cooked in this dish. But any firm-fleshed fish, such as red-fish, red snapper, tilefish, catfish, or cod, will do. Pair this soup with a green salad and some crusty bread and you have a memorable meal.

In a large pan, melt the butter. Add the celery, onion, thyme, pepper flakes, and lemon zest. Cook until the vegetables are softened, stirring once, for about 20 minutes. Stir in the flour a little at a time. Gradually stir in the stock and milk. Cover and simmer until just bubbling and thick, stirring occasionally, about 5 to 10 minutes.

Add the seafood or fish, cover and cook until the fish is opaque, about 5 minutes. Season with sherry, salt, and pepper. Garnish lightly with bell peppers and paprika.

INGREDIENTS

1 Tbsp butter

3–4 shallots, chopped fine

2 celery stalks, chopped fine

5 cups/1.2 1/2 pt water

1 bay leaf

2 salmon steaks (about 450 g/1 lb total weight)

2 potatoes (about 450 g/1 lb), diced

1¼ cups/300 ml/½ pt light cream

ground black pepper

200 g/7 oz smoked salmon, cut in small pieces

1 Tbsp chopped fresh dill

1 Tbsp snipped fresh chives

SMOKED SALMON CHOWDER
SERVES 6

Melt the butter in a heavy pan over medium-low heat. Add the shallots and celery, and sweat until slightly softened. Add the water and bay leaf, cover, and simmer gently for 10 minutes.

Add the salmon steaks and poach for 10 minutes over low heat, covered. Transfer to a plate and allow the fish to cool slightly. Discard the salmon skin and bones, and flake the flesh coarsely.

Meanwhile, stir the potatoes into the cooking liquid and simmer for 15 to 20 minutes, partially covered, until they are tender.

Add the cream to the chowder, season with pepper, and simmer for about 5 minutes to heat through. Stir in the poached salmon, smoked salmon pieces, and herbs, and continue cooking for 5 minutes. Taste and adjust the seasoning, and ladle into warm soup plates or bowls. Serve with fresh bread.

CRAB-CORN CHOWDER

SERVES 4

A favorite recipe, this soup has a wonderfully rich taste and makes an ideal lunch or light supper.

In a large pan over low heat, melt the butter. Sauté the onion, celery, and garlic until wilted, about 5 minutes.

Add the shellfish stock and wine or chicken stock, and bring to a boil. Add the corn and spices. Return to a boil, then reduce the heat, and simmer, uncovered, about 20 minutes.

Stir in the half-and-half and continue simmering for 10 minutes but do not boil. Whisk in the sour cream. Add the crab meat, parsley, and scallions, and heat just enough to warm the crab. Do not allow to boil.

INGREDIENTS

2 Tbsp butter

½ onion, chopped

1 celery stalk, chopped fine

1 garlic clove, minced

1½ cups/360 ml/12 floz shellfish stock (see page 14)

½ cup/120 ml/4 floz dry white wine or chicken stock
(see page 18)

1 cup/100 g/4 oz fresh or frozen corn kernels

¼ tsp dried thyme

½ tsp salt

a pinch cayenne pepper

¼ tsp white pepper

1 cup/100 g/4 oz half-and-half

½ cup/120 ml/4 floz sour cream

225 g/½ lb crab meat

1 Tbsp chopped fresh parsley

2 scallions, chopped

ROASTED PUMPKIN AND SMOKED MUSSEL SOUP

SERVES 6

A luxurious soup that is just as good for a lazy lunch or as a sophisticated appetizer.

Preheat a 220°C/425°F oven. Cut the pumpkin or squash into slices about 1½ to 2 inches/3.75-5 cm wide and place them in a roasting pan. You will need 6 slices. Season lightly with pepper then brush the flesh with olive oil. Bake in the preheated oven for about 30 minutes, until tender. Scoop the flesh from the skin and place to one side.

Heat 2 tablespoons of olive oil in a large pan; add the leek, celery, and carrot, and cook slowly for a further minute. Add the pumpkin or squash flesh to the pan with the cilantro, thyme and bay leaf, then pour in the stock. Bring the soup to a boil, then cover, and simmer slowly for 35 to 40 minutes.

Allow the soup to cool slightly then purée until smooth in a blender or food processor. Rinse the pan then return the soup to it with the milk bring slowly to simmering point. Season well with salt and pepper, then add the smoked mussels, and heat for another minute or two. Serve garnished with parsley, and warm bread.

INGREDIENTS

½ small pumpkin or 1 medium firm-fleshed squash (about 450 g/1 lb)
salt and ground black pepper
3 Tbsp olive oil
1 leek, sliced fine
2 celery stalks, trimmed and sliced
1 carrot, sliced
2 tsp ground cilantro
3–4 sprigs fresh thyme
1 bay leaf
3 cups/729 g/24 floz well-flavored vegetable stock
1¾ cups/420 ml/14 floz milk
125 g/5½ oz smoked mussels

INGREDIENTS

3 Tbsp olive oil

2 onions, chopped

3 garlic cloves, chopped

1 red bell pepper, chopped

about 1 tsp Harissa (purchased)

¼ tsp crushed saffron threads

¼–½ tsp ground cinnamon

¼–½ tsp ground cumin

1 fennel bulb, diced, feathery fronds
reserved

2 large potatoes, chopped

CHUNKY TUNISIAN FISH SOUP

SERVES 6 – 8

This is a substantial fish soup. Any selection of fish and shellfish can be used except oily fish such as mackerel and sardines. If you like, you can use the heads, tails, skin, and bones to make fish stock for the soup.

Heat the oil in a large frying pan, then fry the onion until softened but not colored. Add the garlic and red bell pepper, cook for 2 to 3 minutes, then stir in the Harissa, spices, fennel, potatoes, lemon juice, and stock or water. Bring to a boil then simmer for about 20 minutes until the potatoes are almost cooked. Add the fish, tomatoes, herbs, seasoning, and water as necessary, and cook gently until the fish is tender.

Serve sprinkled with the reserved fennel fronds and accompanied by warmed crusty bread.

MEDITERRANEAN FISH SOUP

SERVES 8

Many versions of this soup, Bouillabaisse, can be found along the Mediterranean coast. Almost any combination of fish and shellfish can be used, but strongly-flavored oily fish are best avoided.

Cut the fish fillets into bite-sized pieces. Trim off any thin ragged bits and reserve for the stock. Put the fish into a large bowl with 2 tablespoons of the olive oil, the orange zest, garlic, saffron, and Pernod. Turn to coat well. Peel the shrimp and reserve the shells. Cover and chill the shrimp and the fish separately.

For the stock, rinse the fish heads, bones, and trimmings under cold running water to remove any blood. Heat the olive oil in a large nonreactive pan or flameproof casserole. Add the leeks, onion, and bell pepper, and cook over medium heat, stirring occasionally, until the onion starts to soften, about 5 minutes.

Add the reserved shrimp shells, fish heads, bones, and trimmings, and continue cookng for 2 minutes. Stir in the tomatoes, garlic, *bouquet garni*, orange zest, saffron, and water (top up if necessary to cover the ingredients). Bring to a boil, skimming off the foam as it rises, then reduce the heat, and simmer gently,

covered, for 30 minutes, skimming once or twice. Strain the stock.

To finish the fish soup, heat the remaining tablespoon of olive oil in a deep sauté pan or wide flameproof casserole over medium heat. Cook the chopped fennel and onion until the onion starts to soften, about 5 minutes, then add the strained stock. Bring to a boil, add the potatoes, and cook for 5 minutes.

Reduce the heat to medium-low and add the fish, starting with the thickest pieces and putting in the thinner ones after 2 to 3 minutes. Add the shrimp and scallops, and continue simmering gently until all the seafood is cooked (opaque throughout).

Transfer the fish, shellfish, and potatoes to a warm tureen or soup plates. Taste for seasoning and ladle the soup over. Serve with croutons spread with *rouille*.

COOK'S TIP

You can prepare the rouille and croutons in advance and make the stock for the soup early in the day while the fish fillets marinate. Then the final assembly isn't too difficult.

INGREDIENTS

1.4 kg/3 lb firm white fish fillets, such as sea bass, snapper, and monkfish

3 Tbsp olive oil

shredded zest of 1 orange (unwaxed or scrubbed)

1 garlic clove, minced

a pinch of saffron threads

2 Tbsp Pernod

675 g/1½ lb large shrimp

1 small fennel bulb, chopped fine

1 large onion, chopped fine

225 g/8 oz small new potatoes, sliced

350 g/12 oz sea scallops, rinsed

Croutons

Rouille

Stock

900 g -1.4 kg/2–3 lb fish heads, bones, and trimmings

2 Tbsp olive oil

2 leeks, sliced

1 onion, halved and sliced

1 red bell pepper, cored and sliced

675 g/1½ lb ripe tomatoes, cored and quartered

4 garlic cloves, sliced

bouquet garni (thyme sprigs, parsley, and bay leaf)

rind of 1 orange (unwaxed or scrubbed), removed with a vegetable peeler

2–3 pinches saffron threads

10 cups/2.4 l/4 pt water

143

CHAPTER FIVE

POULTRY AND GAME

TASTY RECIPES RANGING FROM
A TRADITIONAL CHICKEN
SOUP TO MORE ADVENTUROUS
SPICY DISHES FROM THE EAST.

SMOKED CHICKEN AND LENTIL SOUP

SERVES 4

INGREDIENTS

25 g/1 oz butter

2 leeks, split and sliced thin

2 carrots, chopped fine

1 large onion, chopped fine

1 garlic clove, minced

1 cup/100 g/4 oz dried lentils
(preferably *Puy*)

4 cups/1 1/3¼ pt chicken stock

bouquet garni (thyme sprigs, celery leaves,
sage, and bay leaf)

Lentils are often paired with smoked meats as they seem to give a pleasing element of richness.

Melt the butter in a large pan or stockpot over medium heat. Add the leeks, carrots, onion, and garlic, and cook for 4 to 5 minutes until slightly softened, stirring frequently.

Rinse and drain the lentils, and check for any small stones. Add to the vegetables with the stock and *bouquet garni*. Bring to a boil, reduce the heat to medium-low, and simmer for about 30 minutes, or until the lentils are just tender.

Add the chicken, season to taste with salt and pepper, and continue cooking for 15 minutes. Remove the bouquet garni and ladle into a warm tureen or bowls.

CHINESE CHICKEN AND CORN SOUP

SERVES 6

This Chinese soup is appreciated around the world. The delicate flavors and subtle spicing make it an approachable and suitably light appetizer for entertaining, not to be reserved just for Asian meals.

Put the stock in a large pan with the chicken, onion, carrot, celery, ginger, and bouquet garni. Bring to a boil over medium-high heat, skimming off any foam as it rises to the surface. Reduce the heat to medium-low and simmer, partially covered, for 30 to 40 minutes, or until the chicken is tender. Strain the stock, remove the chicken and discard the vegetables. Shred the chicken.

Cut the kernels from the corn, if using, without cutting down to the cob. With the back of a knife, scrape the cobs to extract the milky liquid from the base of the kernels.

Combine the strained stock, half the scallions, and the corn kernels and their liquid, if available, in the pan, and season with salt and white pepper. Bring to a boil slowly over medium heat and boil gently for 5 minutes.

Stir the cornstarch into 3 tablespoons cold water until dissolved and pour into the soup, stirring constantly. Cook, stirring, until the soup thickens, about 5 minutes. Slowly pour the egg whites into the soup while stirring vigorously. Add the ham and shredded chicken, and heat through, 1 to 2 minutes. Ladle into warm bowls and garnish with the remaining scallions.

COOK'S TIP

If using frozen or canned corn, it will not thicken the soup as much as the starchy liquid from fresh corn, so increase the cornstarch to 4 tablespoons.

INGREDIENTS

7½ cups/1.8 l/3 pt chicken stock

2 boneless skinless chicken breasts

1 small onion, chopped rough

1 carrot, chopped rough

1 celery stalk, chopped rough

1 inch/2.5 cm piece fresh ginger root, peeled and sliced

bouquet garni (parsley stems, leek greens, and bay leaf)

4 ears corn, or 2½ cups/250 g/9 oz thawed frozen or canned corn kernels

8 scallions

salt and white pepper

3 Tbsp cornstarch, or 4 Tbsp if using kernels (see Cook's tip)

2 egg whites, beaten with 3 Tbsp water

50 g/2 oz cooked ham, cut into matchstick strips

UDON WITH CURRY SAUCE

SERVES 4

A modern Japanese innovation combining the spicy flavor of a curry sauce, with the smooth texture of udon *noodles.*

Heat the oil in a pan. Fry the chicken for 5 minutes, or until cooked through. Set aside.

Add the onion, and fry until lightly browned. Add the flour and curry powder, and fry for 1 to 2 minutes.

Gradually dissolve the chicken stock cube into the water, add the chutney and raisins, and season with salt and pepper. Simmer for 10 minutes, then stir in the cooked chicken.

Bring plenty of water to a boil in a pan, and add the *udon*. Cook for 3 minutes, and drain. Rinse under cold water, and drain again. Divide into serving bowls.

Meanwhile, heat the broth. Pour the curry sauce over the udon, and pour the broth over the top. Serve immediately.

INGREDIENTS

550 g/1¼ lb parboiled fresh udon

6 cups/1.5 l/2½ pt dashi broth (see page 16)

Curry

2 Tbsp vegetable oil

2 boneless chicken breasts, diced

1 medium-sized onion, sliced

2 Tbsp flour

1–2 tsp curry powder

½ chicken stock cube

1½ cups/360 ml/12 floz water

2 Tbsp chutney

½ cup/50 g/2 oz raisins

salt and ground black pepper

DUMPLING SOUP

SERVES 6

This Korean dumpling soup contains small dumplings filled with water chestnuts, pork, and chicken, like Chinese dim sum.

Put the vegetables and three quarters of the pork, chicken, and shrimp in a food processor. Dice the remaining pork, chicken, and shrimp. Add the soy sauce, sesame oil, and a pinch of Korean chili powder, or cayenne pepper mixed with paprika, to the food processor, and mix to a smooth paste.

Spoon a little of the vegetable mixture into each wonton wrapper. Wet the edges and draw together to make a neat bundle. Pinch the edges together to seal.

Bring the stock to a boil in a pan. Add the dumplings and diced pork, chicken, and shrimp. Simmer for 8 to 10 minutes. Garnish with scallions before serving.

INGREDIENTS

1 carrot, chopped

1 onion, chopped

1 garlic clove, chopped

6 water chestnuts, chopped

100 g/4 oz lean pork

100 g/4 oz chicken

1 cup/100 g/4 oz cooked, shelled shrimp

2 Tbsp soy sauce

1 Tbsp sesame oil

pinch of Korean chili powder, or cayenne pepper mixed with paprika

30 wonton wrappers

9 cups/2.25 l/3¾ pt chicken stock (see page 18)

chopped scallions, to garnish

CHICKEN SOUP WITH HOMEMADE NOODLES

SERVES 6

INGREDIENTS

4 chicken leg quarters, about 800 g/1¾ lb, skinned

8 cups/2 l/3⅓ pt chicken stock

1 celery stalk, roughly chopped

1 carrot, roughly chopped

1 onion, sliced

1 garlic clove, crushed

5 peppercorns

large *bouquet garni* (parsley stems, thyme sprigs and bay leaf)

1 Tbsp butter

125 g/5 oz mushrooms, sliced

2 Tbsp chopped fresh parsley

Noodles

1 cup/140 g/5 oz flour

¼ tsp salt

2 egg yolks

1 tsp extra-virgin olive oil

pinch saffron threads, soaked in 2 Tbsp hot water

For the noodles, put the flour and salt into a food processor fitted with a steel blade and pulse to combine. In a small bowl, beat together the egg yolks and oil, strain in the saffron liquid and beat to mix; discard the threads. With the machine running, pour in the egg yolk mixture and continue running until it all comes together and forms a ball which leaves the bowl virtually clean. If this doesn't happen and the dough seems a bit sticky, add 2 tablespoons of flour and continue kneading in the food processor until it forms a ball and the dough does not stick to your hands. Wrap and chill for at least 30 minutes.

Divide the dough into quarters and roll out on a lightly floured surface as thinly as possible, less than ¹⁄₁₆ inch/15 mm, and cut into diamond shapes about 1½ inches/4 cm on each side. Alternatively, use a pasta machine to roll the dough into wide strips and cut them into noodles about ⅜ inch/6.5 cm wide. Let the noodles dry in a single layer on floured wire racks or baking trays for about 1 hour. (If making ahead, leave to dry for about 3 hours and store in a plastic bag, refrigerated, for up to 1 day.)

Put the chicken in a large saucepan with the stock, celery, carrot, onion, garlic, peppercorns and bouquet garni. Bring just to a boil over medium-high heat, skimming off the foam as it rises to the surface. Reduce the heat to medium-low and simmer, partially covered, for about 45 minutes, or until the chicken is tender, skimming as needed.

Remove the chicken from the stock and set aside to cool. Continue simmering the stock, uncovered, for about 30 minutes. When the chicken is cool enough to handle, take the meat from the bones and cut into bite-sized pieces. Strain the stock and remove as much fat as possible; discard the *bouquet garni* and vegetables.

Melt the butter in a large saucepan or flameproof casserole over medium heat. Add the mushrooms and 1 tablespoon of water and cook until lightly browned, stirring frequently. Add the stock and bring to a boil. Stir in the noodles and boil gently for 10 minutes. Return the chicken to the stock and continue cooking for 5–10 minutes longer, or until the noodles are tender. Ladle the soup into warm shallow bowls and sprinkle with parsley.

TURKEY CHILI

SERVES 6

INGREDIENTS

1 Tbsp butter

450 g/1 lb skinless boneless turkey, finely chopped or minced

1 onion, finely chopped

2 celery stalks, finely chopped

1 green bell pepper, cored, seeded and finely chopped

2 garlic cloves, minced

1 green chili pepper, cored, seeded and finely chopped

4 cups/1 1/1½ pt turkey or chicken stock

½ tsp chili powder, or to taste (optional)

4 Tbsp extra-virgin olive oil

½ cup/50 g/2 oz blanched almonds

½ cup/50 g/2 oz stoned green olives

salt and freshly ground pepper

1 bunch parsley, stems removed

Chili comes in all colors and this green, relatively mild chili has a creamy richness and appealing complexity.

Melt the butter in a flameproof casserole or large saucepan over medium heat. Add the turkey and cook, stirring frequently, until lightly browned, about 5 minutes. Stir in the onion, celery and green pepper, and cook until softened. Add the garlic and chili pepper, and continue cooking for 2–3 minutes, stirring constantly.

Stir in the stock and bring just to a boil.

Reduce the heat to medium-low and simmer for 5 minutes. Taste and add chili powder if you like it hotter.

Meanwhile, put the oil, almonds, olives and half the parsley in a food processor fitted with a steel blade and process until puréed. Stir the green purée into the soup, season with salt and pepper to taste and simmer, covered, for 20 minutes.

Finely chop the remaining parsley. Ladle the chili into a warm tureen or bowls and sprinkle with chopped parsley.

THAI-SPICED CHICKEN CHOWDER

SERVES 4

A spicy soup that is a meal in itself. Peel the outer skin from the lemon grass then flatten slightly with the blade of a knife before chopping fine.

Heat the oil in a large pan; add the chicken and 7-spice and cook quickly until the chicken begins to brown. Stir in the lemon grass and potato, then add the liquids. Bring the chowder slowly to a boil, then cover, and simmer for 20 minutes.

Stir the scallions into the chowder with the peas; return to a boil then continue cooking over a medium-heat for a further 5 minutes.

Add the satay sauce or peanut butter to the chowder just before serving. Remove from the heat and stir until melted. Season to taste, then serve, garnished with a spoonful of cream if desired.

INGREDIENTS

1–2 Tbsp peanut or sunflower oil

2 small, boneless chicken breasts, skinned and shredded

2 tsp Thai 7-spice seasoning

1 stalk lemon grass, chopped fine

2 medium potatoes, diced

2⅔ cups/640 ml/1 pt chicken or vegetable stock

1¾ cups/420 ml/14 floz milk

3–4 scallions, trimmed and sliced fine

1 cup/200 g/8 oz frozen peas

1–2 Tbsp satay sauce or peanut butter

salt and ground black pepper

1–2 Tbsp heavy cream, to garnish

GAME BIRD CONSOMME WITH POACHED QUAIL EGGS

SERVES 4

This is not a classic consommé, as it is not clarified. Cooking it slowly is an easy and effective method to achieve a relatively clear stock and retain the delicate flavor that would be lost in the clarification process.

Put the carcass(es), onion, carrots, parsnip, leek, garlic, peppercorns, and *bouquet garni* in a stockpot or large heavy pan. Add the stock and enough cold water to cover the ingredients by 1 inch/2.5 cm. Bring slowly to a boil over medium heat, skimming the foam that rises to the surface often. Reduce the heat to low and simmer for 1½ to 2 hours. Strain the stock through a strainer lined with damp cheesecloth into a bowl and if any meat can be picked off the carcass(es), reserve it. Cool the stock and chill for several hours or overnight. Skim off any congealed fat and blot the surface with a paper towel to remove any remaining fat.

Bring a small pan of salted water to a boil and poach the quail eggs, a few at a time, for 2 to 3 minutes, or until done as you like them. Remove with a slotted spoon to a bowl of tepid water to stop further cooking. Trim off any untidy bits of white.

Bring the stock just to a boil and reduce the heat to medium-low. Taste and season with a little salt, if needed, and stir in the sherry. If the stock is bland, reduce it slightly with a fresh *bouquet garni*.

Place the poached eggs in warm shallow soup plates, ladle over the consommé, and garnish with chervil or parsley leaves.

INGREDIENTS

1 large game bird carcass, such as pheasant or duck, or 3–4 small ones, such as pigeon or quail, raw or cooked and trimmed of excess fat

1 large onion, quartered

2 carrots, chopped coarse

1 parsnip, chopped coarse

1 leek, sliced

2–4 garlic cloves, crushed

1 Tbsp black peppercorns

bouquet garni (thyme sprigs, parsley stems, tarragon or sage leaves, and bay leaf)

3 cups/720 ml/24 floz cold chicken stock

salt (optional)

2–3 Tbsp dry sherry

8 quail eggs

fresh chervil or Italian parsley, to garnish

159

SOBA WITH CHICKEN

SERVES 4

The chicken used in this dish should be marinated for as long as you can to extract as much flavor from the sauce as possible, so don't be tempted to cut down on the times, below, which should be treated as a minimum.

Marinate the chicken in the soy sauce for at least 15 minutes. Put the chicken, leek, and *dashi* broth in a saucepan, bring to a boil, and simmer for 10 to 15 minutes, or until the chicken is cooked. Occasionally skim off the scum which will form on top.

Boil plenty of water in a large pan, and add the soba. Cook for 5 to 6 minutes. Rinse well under water, and drain thoroughly. Divide the noodles into four bowls.

Pour the broth with chicken and leek into the bowls. Garnish with the sprouts. Sprinkle with the Thai-7 spice, and then serve at once.

INGREDIENTS

6 cups/1.5 1/2 ¾ pt *dashi* broth (see page 16)
400 g/14 oz dried *soba*

Topping

3 boneless chicken breasts, sliced on a slant into bite-sized pieces
2 Tbsp Japanese soy sauce
1 leek, sliced thin diagonally
alfalfa sprouts, to garnish
Thai-7 spice seasoning

TARRAGON CHICKEN CONSOMME WITH CHICKEN QUENELLES

SERVES 6

A richly flavored, sparkling clear consommé is considered a true indicator of culinary skill. Although it is relatively expensive and time-consuming, it is worth making the effort at least once.

Finely chop the chicken breast in a food processor or by hand. Put in a large pan with the leeks, onion, celery, parsley, and dried tarragon. Add the egg whites, mix to combine and stir in the stock. Set over high heat and stir almost continuously as the mixture comes to a boil. When it begins to tremble, reduce the heat to low, and simmer very gently, without stirring or disturbing it, for 30 minutes. Carefully lift off about a third of the solid covering, using a slotted spoon, and ladle the clarified stock through a strainer lined with damp cheesecloth. (Discard the solid matter.)

For the chicken quenelles, cut the chicken breast into large pieces, put in a food processor fitted with a steel blade and process until smooth. Add the egg white and tarragon, and mix until combined. Add the cream by spoonfuls. Do not overprocess or the mixture will become warm and the cream will not be readily absorbed. Season generously and chill for at least 15 minutes.

Bring a pan of salted water to a simmer. Using two teaspoons, shape the chicken mixture into small ovals and drop into the water a few at a time. Poach for about 2 minutes until they float and feel firm to the touch. Drain on clean paper towels.

Bring the consommé just to a boil over medium-high heat. Divide the quenelles among warmed shallow soup plates, ladle over the consommé, and sprinkle with a little chopped tarragon. Serve immediately.

INGREDIENTS

1 skinless; boneless chicken breast

2 small leeks, chopped fine

1 onion, chopped fine

1 celery stalk, chopped fine

3–4 sprigs of fresh parsley, chopped fine

2 tsp dried tarragon

2 egg whites

10 cups/2.4 l/4 pt strong fat-free chicken stock

chopped fresh tarragon leaves, to garnish

Chicken quenelles

1 skinless; boneless chicken breast, well chilled

1 egg white

1 Tbsp chopped fresh tarragon

4 Tbsp heavy cream, well chilled

salt and ground black pepper

freshly grated nutmeg

INGREDIENTS

1 onion, halved

2 celery stalks, including leaves, diced

2 carrots, diced

1 parsnip, diced

5 garlic cloves,. peeled

1.4 kg/3 lb stewing chicken

7 cups/1.7 1/3 pt water

½ tsp fresh basil, minced

½ tsp curry powder

a dash of hot pepper sauce

1 tsp minced cilantro

salt and ground black pepper

SPICY CHICKEN SOUP
SERVES 4

This soup is anything but bland—it has a well-seasoned, true chicken flavor and the vegetables added toward the end have freshness, color, and lots of nutrients. Try adding some of the chicken, shredded or diced, and some noodles for a meal-in-a-dish.

Divide the vegetables in half and place in 2 bowls or on sheets of wax paper. Place the garlic, chicken, and half the vegetables in a Dutch oven or stockpot. Add water to cover the chicken, then the basil, curry powder, hot pepper sauce, cilantro, and salt and pepper to taste. Bring to a boil, then immediately reduce the heat, and simmer uncovered for about 2 hours.

Skim all the fat off the top of the stockpot and strain the soup. Chill the cooked chicken for later use.

Add the remaining vegetables to the soup. Simmer for 10 minutes, or until the vegetables are tender. Serve.

INGREDIENTS

4 chicken pieces

½ Spanish onion, chopped fine

7 cups/1.7 l/3 pt chicken stock

2 Tbsp short-grain rice

salt

1½ Tbsp lemon juice

4 Tbsp chopped fine mint

CHICKEN, LEMON, AND MINT SOUP

SERVES 4

Traditionally this soup would have been made from an old hen that had ceased to lay. The bird would therefore be tough and require long, gentle poaching to make it tender. It would have been cooked in water but by the end of the cooking time the liquid would be well-flavored and silky-textured. In this modern version, lemon and mint give the soup a clean, fresh taste.

Put the chicken pieces into a heavy flameproof casserole into which they fit comfortably. Add the onion and stock, bring to a simmering point, and remove the scum from the surface. Lower the heat so the liquid barely moves, cover, and cook for 3 minutes. Add the rice and salt, and cook for a further 30 minutes.

Remove the casserole from the heat and leave until the chicken pieces are cool enough to handle. Lift the chicken pieces from the casserole. Discard the skin and remove the meat from the bones. Cut the meat into short strips, return to the casserole, stir in the lemon juice and bring to a boil.

Divide the mint among four soup bowls and ladle in the soup, distributing the chicken flesh and rice evenly.

CURRIED CHICKEN CHOWDER

SERVES 4

The subtle curry and slightly tart apple flavors give this soup a pleasing complexity that makes it suitable for the most elegant occasions. The strength of curry powders varies, so use your own judgment, but it should not dominate.

Melt the butter in a large, heavy pan over medium heat. Add the onion and garlic. Cook, stirring frequently, until the vegetables start to soften, about 5 minutes. Stir in the flour and curry powder and cook for 2 minutes. Stir in the carrots, celery, potato, and stock. Bring to a boil, stirring frequently. Add the *bouquet garni* and season with salt and pepper.

Reduce the heat to medium-low and simmer, stirring occasionally, until the vegetables are almost tender, about 20 minutes. Add the apple and chicken, and continue cooking for about 10 minutes, or until the apple is tender. Remove the *bouquet garni.*

Stir in the cream, taste and adjust the seasoning, and heat through. Ladle into warm bowls and garnish with chives.

INGREDIENTS

2 Tbsp butter

1 onion, chopped fine

1 garlic clove, minced

3 Tbsp flour

1 tsp curry powder

2 small carrots, halved lengthwise and sliced thin

1 celery stalk, sliced thin

1 potato, diced

4 cups1 l/1½ pt chicken stock

bouquet garni (parsley, thyme sprigs, and bay leaf)

salt and ground black pepper

1 dessert apple, peeled, cored, and diced

2 cups/150 g/6 oz cubed cooked chicken

4–6 Tbsp heavy cream

2 Tbsp snipped fresh chives, to garnish

BOILED RICE SOUP WITH CHICKEN

SERVES 4

The traditional and universal Thai breakfast is tasty and nourishing. It is made with ground pork, and an optional extra is an egg cracked straight into the dish just before serving; it partly poaches in the hot soup.

Boil the chicken stock in a pan. Add the chicken, rice, cabbage, salt, and pepper; boil the chicken until cooked, about 8 to 10 minutes. Add the celery and scallion, and then remove from the heat immediately.

Pour into bowls and sprinkle with the fried garlic. Serve with the *phrik dong* and fish sauce in separate bowls.

INGREDIENTS

7 cups/1.7 l/2¾ pt chicken stock
300 g/11 oz boneless skinned chicken breasts, cut across into thin slices
4 cups/200 g/8 oz cooked rice
1 Tbsp chopped pickled cabbage
1 tsp salt
1 tsp ground white pepper
1 cup/100g/4 oz celery, sliced fine
2 scallions, sliced
⅓ cup/50 g/2 oz garlic cloves, unpeeled and fried until soft
½ cup/50 g/2 oz *phrik dong* (sliced red chile with vinegar)
2 Tbsp fish sauce

CHICKEN AND CHILE SOUP

SERVES 4 – 6

Heat the oil in a large pan and fry the curry paste gently for 3 minutes, stirring occasionally.

Add the stock with the coconut milk, chiles, lemon grass, lime leaves, and ginger. Bring to a boil and boil for 3 minutes. Reduce the heat, then add the chicken strips, and simmer gently for 5 to 10 minutes, or until the chicken is cooked.

Add the green beans and cucumber with the rice and honey. Simmer for a further 5 minutes.

Stir in the cream, if using, and serve.

INGREDIENTS

1 tsp oil

1 tsp green curry paste

2½ cups/600 ml/1 pt chicken stock

⅔ cup coconut milk

1 or 2 bird's eye (Thai) chiles, seeded and chopped

2 lemon grass stalks, outer leaves removed and chopped fine

4 kaffir lime leaves

1 inch/2.5 cm piece ginger root, peeled and shredded

350 g/12 oz chicken breasts, skinned and cut into thin strips

1 cup/100 g/4 oz green beans, trimmed and cut into short pieces

3 inch/7.5 cm pieces cucumber, peeled if preferred and cut into strips

½ cup/75 g/3 oz cooked fragrant rice

1–2 tsp honey

4 Tbsp light cream (optional)

CHICKEN AND VEGETABLE SOUP

SERVES 6

Put the chicken pieces and stock into a large pan, and bring to a boil over high heat. Skim off the foam with a large spoon, then reduce the heat, partially cover, and simmer for 45 minutes.

Skim the fat from the soup. Add the tomatoes, corn, yams, potatoes, pumpkin, peas, hot peppers, salt, and freshly ground black pepper, and bring to a boil. Reduce the heat, and simmer for about 20 minutes or until the chicken and vegetables are cooked.

Taste the soup, adjusting the seasoning if necessary. Stir in the chives, then serve immediately.

INGREDIENTS

1.4 kg/3 lb chicken, cut into 8 pieces

15½ cups/3.8 l/6¼ pt chicken stock

4 large tomatoes, peeled, seeded, and chopped; or 2 x 450 g/1 lb cans chopped tomatoes, drained

2 medium-sized corn cobs, cut into 3 inch/7.5 cm pieces

2 medium yams, peeled and chopped into 1 inch/2.5 cm thick slices

100 g/¼ lb pumpkin, peeled and diced

¾ cup/150 g/6 oz fresh or frozen green peas

Chapter Six

Meat

BEEF, LAMB AND SAUSAGE
FEATURE IN THESE
MOUTH-WATERING AND
OFTEN UNUSUAL SOUPS
FROM AROUND THE WORLD.

LAMB AND VEGETABLE SOUP WITH VERMICELLI

SERVES 6

Variations of this thickened vermicelli soup can be found throughout North Africa. The lamb is simmered to become tender and succulent.

Heat the oil in a large pan, then cook the onions, garlic, bell peppers, and lamb, stirring occasionally, for 10 minutes. Add the bones, stock, seasoning, chile, tomatoes, apricots, and mint and bring just to a boil then simmer for about 1¼ to 1½ hours until the lamb is very tender.

Bring to a boil, add the vermicelli and cook for 5 minutes until tender. Pour the soup into a warmed tureen, stir in the lemon juice and garnish with chopped parsley and mint.

INGREDIENTS

3 Tbsp olive oil
4 onions, chopped
3 cloves garlic, minced
3 red bell peppers, chopped
675 g/1½ lb lean lamb, cubed
2 lamb bones, cracked
10 cups/2.4 l/4 pt meat stock or water
salt and ground black pepper
a pinch of crushed dried red chiles
4 tomatoes, chopped
½ cup/30 g/2 oz dried apricots
1–1½ Tbsp chopped fresh mint
½ cup vermicelli

INGREDIENTS

450 g/1 lb sweet Italian sausages

1 Tbsp olive oil

1 large onion, finely chopped

2 garlic cloves, minced

1 fennel bulb, finely chopped

½ red or yellow bell pepper, seeded and finely chopped

450 g/1 lb zucchini, coarsely grated

6 cups/1.5 l/2½ pt brown chicken or beef stock

1 tsp chopped fresh marjoram, or ¼ tsp dried

1 tsp chopped fresh thyme, or ¼ tsp dried

bay leaf

salt and freshly ground pepper

Lemon-garlic seasoning

grated zest of ½ lemon (unwaxed or scrubbed)

1 garlic clove, minced

2 Tbsp chopped parsley

ITALIAN SAUSAGE AND ZUCCHINI SOUP

SERVES 4–6

This soup emphasizes the fennel used to flavor many Italian sausages. If other sausages are used, add a pinch of fennel seeds to the soup. The lemon, garlic, and parsley seasoning, or gemolata, a traditional garnish for stews and seafood, brings a pleasant zing to the soup.

Put the sausages in a frying pan and set over medium heat. Cook until well browned, turning to color evenly. Remove and drain on paper towels. Cut into slices.

Heat the oil in a heavy saucepan or flameproof casserole over medium-high heat. Add the onion, garlic, fennel and pepper, and cook for 3–4 minutes, stirring occasionally, until slightly softened.

Add the zucchini, stock and herbs. Stir in the sliced sausages, reduce the heat to low and simmer for about 20 minutes. Add a little stock or water if you like a thinner soup. Season to taste with salt, if needed, and pepper. Discard the bay leaf.

COOK'S TIP

This is a good way to use a large zucchini. If the skin is very tough, peel before grating.

ARAB LAMB AND GARBANZO SOUP

SERVES 4 – 6

If using dried garbanzos, cook over medium heat in boiling unsalted water to cover generously until tender, about 1½ hours. Drain.

Heat the oil in a flameproof casserole or large heavy pan over high heat. Add enough of the lamb to cover the base of the pan sparsely and cook, stirring frequently, until evenly browned. Remove the browned meat and continue cooking in batches, adding a little more oil if needed. When the last batch is nearly browned, add the onion and garlic, and cook, stirring frequently, for 2 minutes. Return all the meat to the pan and add the wine, if using, water, thyme, oregano, bay leaf, cinnamon, and cumin. Bring just to a boil, skimming off any foam

as it rises to the surface, reduce the heat to low and simmer for about 1½ hours until the meat is very tender. Discard the bay leaf.

Stir in the garbanzos, tomatoes or tomato juice, roasted bell peppers, saffron or turmeric, leek, carrot, and potato, and simmer for 15 minutes. Add the zucchini and beans, and continue simmering for 15 to 20 minutes more, or until all the vegetables are tender. Taste and adjust the seasoning, adding a little Harissa, if you like spicier soup.

Ladle the soup into a warmed tureen or bowls and sprinkle with fresh mint or cilantro.

INGREDIENTS

¾ cup/150 g/6 oz garbanzo beans, soaked overnight and drained, or 1¾ cups canned chickpeas, rinsed and drained

1½–2 Tbsp olive oil

675g/1½ lb boneless lamb shoulder, trimmed of all fat and cut into 1 inch/2.5 cm cubes

1 onion, chopped fine

3 garlic cloves, minced

4 Tbsp dry white wine (optional)

5 cups/1.2 1/2 pt water

¾ tsp dried thyme

¾ tsp dried oregano

1 bay leaf

¼ tsp ground cinnamon

¼ tsp cumin seeds

4 tomatoes, peeled, seeded, and chopped, or 1 cup/240 ml/8 floz tomato juice

2 roasted bell peppers, peeled, seeded, and chopped

¼ tsp ground saffron or turmeric

1 large leek, halved lengthwise and sliced

1 large carrot, diced

1 large potato, diced

2 medium zucchini, halved lengthwise and sliced

⅔ cup/100g/4 oz fresh or thawed frozen green peas

Harissa (hot red pepper paste (purchased)

chopped fresh mint, or cilantro, to garnish

SAUSAGE AND TOMATO SOUP

SERVES 6

This hearty, warming soup is filling enough for a main course. Use good-quality sausages from a reputable delicatessen to be sure of the best results.

Cook the bacon gently in a heavy pan until the fat has been rendered.

Prick the sausages and cook with the bacon for a few minutes, stirring two or three times, before stirring in the onion and garlic. Cook until softened; then add the tomatoes, bay leaf, and stock or water.

Bring to a boil and simmer gently, uncovered, for about 30 minutes.

Remove the sausages and slice, return to the pan, reheat, and season. Serve with firm country bread.

INGREDIENTS

2 slices bacon, chopped

225 g/8 oz garlic-flavored smoked sausage

225 g/8 oz morcela sausage or blood sausage

1 Spanish onion, halved and sliced

2 garlic cloves, crushed

1 kg/2¼ lb well-flavored tomatoes, chopped

1 bay leaf

4¼ cups/1 l/1¾ pt vegetable or chicken stock or water

salt and ground black pepper

firm country bread, to serve

INDEX